T0354688

Opening *the* Cage

Opening *the* Cage

A
collection of
poems

CHLOE DEVIN HARDY

⦿iUniverse®

OPENING THE CAGE
A COLLECTION OF POEMS

iUniverse books may be ordered through booksellers or by contacting:

iUniverse
1663 Liberty Drive
Bloomington, IN 47403
www.iuniverse.com
844-349-9409

ISBN: 978-1-6632-6755-9 (sc)
ISBN: 978-1-6632-6754-2 (e)

Library of Congress Control Number: 2024921200

Print information available on the last page.

iUniverse rev. date: 10/02/2024

About the Author

Chloe has lived a life filled with trauma. At first she let it destroy her. Until she found a counselor who suggested she write to cope with her trauma. This is a collection of the thoughts that were once trapped in her head. She hopes they help you as much as they helped her.

This book starts with the very first poem she ever wrote. At the age of 12 she wrote it as a Father's Day present. The poems continue throughout her high school years. There are poems written during many of the ups and downs within her failed marriage. In the later years they were written in a mixture of addiction, jail, and finally sobriety. These poems encompass all of the pain life has held for her, that she is able to communicate in some way.

Contents

Father's Day

Dad let me guess
Your life is full of stress
I know you lose your temper
But please try to remember
What it was like when you were a kid
And all the things you did
On a motorcycle you wear a leather
On which you let me get a turkey feather
If I had a wish
It would be this:
It would be to make all your dreams come true
Because on Father's Day it's all about you
When we race on the race car track
You flip mine and I flip yours back
When grandma died
We all cried
But know she is here
To share out cheer
So while you drink your beer
I hope you are full of laughter and cheer
Your great to be around, even if your soul is not found
When you are working
You are focusing
Until you're done you don't put a tool down
You're the greatest dad in town.

Used to Be

I used to be special
I used to be your only
you left me for friends
you left me for whores
I turned and ran
I turned and laughed
you looked confused
you looked used
I told more people
I told my parents
you tried to deny
you tried to lie
I wonder now how you are
I wonder now who you are
you've changed for the better
you've changed with every letter
I was sad, I was mad
you think you won, you think I'm done
so I hold a knife, so I hold our life
you try to stop me, you try to love me
I can't be loved, I can't be missed
you've never seen this, you've never experienced
I used to be an angel, I used to be alive
how you told everyone, how you witnessed
I finally did it. I finally died.

Hidden Concept

You don't know her, just a concept
The full picture a little harder to accept
She has yet to learn when to stop the words
But her main focus is to end the hurt
She has a habit of sacrificing herself
Not many are permitted access to her heart on the shelf
To let her guard slip
Is a mistake she cannot commit
Allowing others to bring her down
And once again she is their jester, just another clown
They never saw her true power
They only saw kindness to devour
Torn piece by piece she tried to hold strong
She did her best not to speak against wrong
She did always as she was told
Compromise, let them win…..fold
She followed all of their silly rules
All while enduring the cruel
Then one day she questioned
And their power all came tumbling down
And she emerged broken, but finally free from the crowd

The First to Walk Out

Do you recall the words used?
To form the perfect excuse
The way you casually walked away
Claiming the memory would fade
But the piece you left me
Awakens the memory every day
There is you in the little things
And it takes all of me to react to nothing
Then I hear her plan a future built on you
Somehow after all these years you started anew
I cant help but wonder why I was the game
Just a fake trophy in your name
It took years to not be pissed
Only moments for you to be missed
You want to brag about all the good you've done
But leave out the fiancée and child you left alone

Misconception

When a child is wanted love comes
but yet when it isn't hate runs
when you say you love me its great
but when I say it back I'm crazy
I never wanted to love you
I just do
I forgive everything
to mean something, to you
my heart falls
my hand draws
the last of the picture
you with her
she's beautiful
with lips so full
no one objects
I'm the reject
how could I think
you would blink
tears pour out of my eyes
my lies are at fault, my lies
I hate to be the reason
for the end of our season
but I do love you
as though it's the only statement from me that's true

Sleeping Through The Night

I remember
Remember the pain
Pain I felt
Felt as you touched
Touched my body
Body scarred by you
You and all you do
Do to make me regret
Regret everything that
That you got away with
With you is my soul
Soul you stole
Stole while I wept
Wept over how stupid
Stupid I was for believing
Believing that if I tell
Tell someone what you've done
Done to me
Me, I just might break free
Free of you I cringe
Cringe at the sight
Sight of my freedom
Freedom in nothing but the night
Nights go by without a sound
Sounding the alarm as I sleep

That Girl

She loved you
And it's the truth
You promised forever
You should have lied better
She came to me
For the comforting
Don't tell me you're sorry
No don't you dare worry
Your dumbass got her thinking
Of slinking away
Into nothingness
And its your fault she's doing this
She can't live anymore
She feels like a stupid whore
Thanks for doing that
Now I have to watch her every act
People don't get it
She wants to slit her wrist
But you don't give a shit
Cant you hear her breaking
You should have what with her voice shaking
You're a worthless pig
Luckily I'm not allowed out
I'll show what this is about
I love that girl
The one you love to hurt

7

My Prince

A painful memory
Seeps through me
Of a long time ago
When you decided to go
I knew you would leave
You tried to deceive, it to where
I had not one care
Who told you what to do
Im not about to forgive
Live and let live
Its what everyone says
But no one believes
Can you understand
Why I raise my hand
It was in defense
Of my last request
I asked not to touch him
I think of him as royalty
He is so young
But his eyes were stung
By the words you used
To just abuse
He is a child
So young and mild
Leave him alone
Wreck someone else's home

Prompted

I told you no
No please don't go
Go away from me
Me, I start to plea
Plea for one more chance
Chance I won't mess up
Messed up with you
You act like you wanted me to

9

No Escape

I feel naked
Because you know what I did
He was a nobody
But swore he loved me
So I believed him
Just to see him win
Another girl's love
I hear your cry from above
But its not my problem
I didn't make them
So why do I feel guilty
Why does everyone look to me?
I washed my hands clean
Why is that so mean
I told him goodbye
He chose to cry
To someone else near
Then I hear.....a scream
Of pain it seems
He grabs onto me
I beg to be let free
My shirt starts to rip
He throws me on the bed
Smacks me in the head
Leaves me for dead

Just Leave

All this over a note
I shouldn't have wrote
I didn't do anything
I know what you're thinking
You think I cheated
That I mistreated
My right as his girl
He means all the world
To me but oh well
I guess I'll see you in hell
I'm going there tonight
But I'll be alright
I won't have to cry
Or even ask why
I'll take all their shit
I think it will be worth it
Believe me I'm sorry
I have to leave in a hurry
I want to get the timing right
I have to do this tonight
I know people think it's wrong
But I end this with my only song
I never want to breakdown
In front of a crowd
So I leave
Just let me be

Validation

How? They ask
I seriously don't know
I just need to let go
The world around me cruel
For which I feel like a fool
How could I say
That I'd be okay
You look in my eyes
Knowing that lie
I didn't mean to
Try and hurt you
But I cant go on acting like
Everything will be alright
I just want to walk around
Without my head hanging down
I need someone to tell me not to leave
Someone that will beg and plead
I know how they all think they're right
So maybe I'll do it tonight
A cut here
A cut there
Blood will pour
Just because they think I'm a whore
I don't want much from you
Just say you always knew
That no matter what I do, I love you

Overwhelmed

The way I see it
I can't deal with the shit
So I'll walk away
Pretending to be okay
But really I'm not
Just lost my train of thought
I get back to where I was
And nothing is there
Its completely bare
And all I can think
Is I'm growing weak
Why do I let them win
I should be stronger than them
I can push and pull
But feel like a fool
Or I can sit and grin
Letting them in
I should give up on this
But I would miss
The sound of your voice
Do I have a choice
Is letting go too much
It is compared to your touch
But I want to be free
To finally have something I forgot
To finally let them see that I'm not
What they want me to be

13

Happiness Forbidden

Breaking down I decide
To end the pathetic life
Why should I live
What do I have to give
People think its funny
To see the blood running
This isn't a joke
If you laugh you might choke
Happiness forbidden
The pain I have ridden
I don't let go
I finally say no
But its too late
They've decided my fate
Death is all they say
And leave me to wait
Why do I wait here so long
What the hell did I do wrong
With every word I write
I slip into a night
I won't return
This is the final burn
People might read this
And call me distress
But I'm not really
Really I'm free

14

Love Me

I'm back to normal, you're feelin' crazy
But I don't care and you don't mind
So don't you dare leave me behind
If you love me just tell me
Don't be shy
If you love me just tell me
It'll be alright
When you decide that we'll be alright
Just tap me on the shoulder
I'm sure to roll over
If you love me just tell me
Don't be shy
If you love me just tell me
It'll be alright
Don't tell me I'm nothing
When I kiss you
You can't breathe
If you love me just tell me
Don't be shy
If you love me just tell me
It'll be alright

15

Believe You

Watch for me
See what I see
Don't cry
I'll be alright
Call me crazy, call me insane
Just don't say his name
Because it burns
And it hurts
To hear the words
Say I'm okay and I'll believe you
Even if it is untrue
Tell me something I can believe in
Show me something I can win
Don't be fake
I'm not a mistake
I just can't seem to get it
Why did I let him in
They blame me you know
Calling me a hoe
Just because
He decided to touch me

Long Time Gone

The pain is gone
And hope left long ago
Just because he decided
I was a hoe
You people laugh at me
Because you've never seen it
The way I hide, weak
Maybe I'm different
But at least I admit
So now that I'm here
Let me tell you
My pain, sadness, fear, and self-hatred
Are all a long time gone

Uncertainty

I started to choke
You're such a fucking joke
You love me
But you still want to leave?
Right, should I listen
My eyes glisten
But not over you
My precious boo
See I'm fine
Got another wanting to be mine
So I'll go to him
There now I win
Oh wait you want me back
Must have given you a heart attack
To see me holding his hand
But guess what? Too bad
Guess he loves me
He doesn't want to leave
So just turn around
You stupid fucking clown

Not A Reason

For you I love
To you I give
All of me
Completely
I love you
I need you
Hold me close
I'll miss you most
I will fight
I won't be polite
Why should I be
They took you away from me
I cried so hard
I tried so far
But I feel I failed
Our love still prevailed
You say it's okay
You say you love me today
And I hate to think
Of a reason why
I would let us die

Pathogenic Lips

I hear the lies
Spreads far and wide
With your pathogenic lips
Saying how you did this
I asked you to not touch me
Now I demand that you leave
You told me he wasn't right
That you control me tonight
Well it's funny that you think of this
As I have told you of my bliss
You're not him by far
He wouldn't do this in a fucking car
You say you love me
But ignored my pleas
I have my man
Remove your hands
This body isn't yours
I'm not like those other whores
I know you think I haven't changed
But you're totally wrong, he rearranged
The way I thought
My life before I forgot
Do you think about me everyday
Or only when you're horny
My not so precious friend Tony

My Mistake

From fear I hid
To you I'd give
From pain I'd run
To you i'd come
From regret I'd shake
To you...my mistake
I didn't mean to
Really I didn't want to hurt you
But I did
And I'm sorry for this
I know you hate me
But just listen......please
Then you walk away
Pretending I'm nothing
But deep down
I hold your crown
I hold your heart and soul
And you're scared because you lose control
So you hide the love you feel
And leave me at last for real
Then you see me with him
And it tears you from within
I guess now you know
You shouldn't have let me go

My Love

You left your mark
On my heart
And I tried so hard
To hide the scar
But I still see it now
From when you said how
You could leave me
But you couldn't see
You love me back
And it smacks you in the face
You had to think of how to say
You needed me
So I helped you
And suddenly the blue
Disappeared quickly
Because you kissed me
And held me in your eyes
I try to despise you
But I cant pretend
Or to offend you when
You're my life, my joy, my love
Who I hold nothing above
So hold me closer
Love me longer
Don't let go please for God's sake just don't let go

If I Could

If I could only take it back:
I'd take back the angry words
I'd take back all the hurt
I'd take back all the shoves
But I'd never take back the love
If I could talk to you one last time:
I'd tell you I'm sorry
I'd tell you not to worry
I'd tell you I miss you
and that I'll never forget you
If I could spend one more day:
I'd never let you out of my sight
I'd never want to say goodnight
I'd hold you every second of the day
and I would feel okay
If I could only hear your words:
I would want you to say straighten up
I would want you to say don't give up
I would want you to say I'll be fine
oh if only I had to do it all over again
I would give you the time to do everything
I couldn't before you passed away

23

In Memory Of

I loved you when:
I loved you when you smiled
I loved you when you got wild
I loved you when no one else would
Not always good
I hated you when:
I hated you when you weren't around
I hated you when you were lowered into the ground
I hated you when I had to say good bye
And I still wonder why you had to die
I missed you when:
I missed you when the first tear fell
I missed you when the nurse talked about heaven and hell
I missed you when I left that day
Why couldn't you have stayed?
I think about you when:
I think about you when I sing
I think about you when I'm doing nothing
I think about you when I dream
This is a dream too it seems
You can't really be gone
For I still hear your sweet song

No Mercy

I have no mercy for you
So don't turn to me when you're blue
You let me get hurt so bad
And now you better believe I'm mad
I write to keep my mind clear
If not you would disappear
To never utter another word
About how much you hurt
She still hates me for that day
You came to kill me
Can't you see I'm over the fear
Of seeing you standing there
You block my way like I'm weak
But are surprised when I slap your cheek?
You'd never know unless Ii said
I truly wish you were dead

If......

If I were to fall would you catch me?
Most likely you would
If I were o cry would you wonder why?
I hope you would
If I were to act angry would you be sorry?
I think you would
But if I were to call would you answer?
I'm pretty sure you won't
If you were to fall
I would fall catching you
If you were to cry
I would ask so many questions I'd sound crazy
If you were to act angry
I would feel so sorry no one could be sorrier
And if you were to call
Ii would pickup without a second thought
If we were to fall who would pick us up?
Pretty sure only us
If we were to cry who would wonder why?
Pretty sure only us
If we were to act angry who would be sorry?
Pretty sure no one
If we were to call on someone who would answer?
I hope we'd get an answer from each other

The Storm

The clouds gather quickly
The storm is thickening
And I hear the thunder
As it is full of hunger
And I feel a chill
And I feel the need to kill
But I hide in the shadow
While the puddles are shallow
And I stay there and think
So I won't blink
I have to watch the storm
In its most beautiful form
Because if I turn away
It will go quickly
And it must stay here
So Ii don't have to fave my fear

Head Games

You say you love me
And need me near
Yet when I come close
You disappear
I try to be calm
And tell myself nothing's wrong
But then I see
Yet again you're gone
I don't know how to act
And I don't want to be attacked
So I just sit there
And try not to react
But you say you missed me
And I think it's right again
So I reach out
Just to grab your hand
But you pull back
Saying that I've changed too much
And I start to feel low
Because you once again tell me to hush
But now I know the game
So it's time I play
So I say I'm sorry and I love you
And you say you need me near
And then just like that I disappear

28

No Voice

No voice of my own
I start to let go
No one to catch me
I fall all alone
All the hatred in the world
And I start to lose control
All the pain I can't stand
I can't obey the commands
Some of the power
I had once longed for
Some of the love you give
I realize all I need to live
I now have a voice
And someone will catch me
I now understand the hatred
And I can finally stand the pain
If you ask me I do have the power
And I still have all of your love

Open Canvas

An open canvas
Because I don't paint distress
You can't understand
Why I refuse your command
But why should I obey you
The way you treat me is nothing new
Your shouts mean nothing now
I'm supposed to say sorry but how
I'm not sorry for us
No need to fight and cuss
I'm over that heart break
You see you were my mistake
I should have never come back
To your violent attacks
So the canvas isn't blank anymore
It's full of the pride, of mine, I earned

Final Adieu

Out of sight out of mind
I wish your memory was so kind
I've thought myself crazy for you
And all I get back is a final adieu
You pass me by like air
And I know in my heart you just don't care
I wish it was easy to forget
But all I do is regret
Regret the touches, the kisses, the words
But most of all I regret my own hurt
I know you don't really give a damn
But if you did I don't think I can
I'm done trying the fates and loving you
I just want you to know this is my final adieu

Hurt

Bruises fade
Hurt never goes
If this is fate
I'll never know
Its hard to tell
If it was meant to be
If this is hell
Why can't I see
I wonder if you knew
How I truly feel
Could you be true
Could it have been real
It doesn't matter I guess
Considering you're gone
I wish I could fix the mess
But all I can do is move on

Broken Hope

Standing together
But miles apart
I thought you said forever
But you broke my heart
It didn't take much
Just more than I expected
Maybe a harsh touch
And I felt rejected
Knowing you saw so little
And hearing everything you felt
Makes my heart fall to the middle
Between breaking and wanting to melt
I can't be perfect
Or even close
This is your effect
Sorry I don't miss you the most
But you hurt me so much
And it made me realize I was a fool
To hurt me means you had control
So I guess its all just broken hope

Release Me

With one word I cringe
A simple goodbye
As I hang on the fringe
It hurt my pride
To know I failed at this
But I won't be brave
And I won't have you to miss
For I no longer crave
The tender touch I know you possess
I just want the release
For that caress
That's all I really need.

Stale Fairytale

You say with time it will stop
I wonder if it ever was
You say you blame the cop
But I know it was all because
I gave all of me to you
Hoping something would show
But it made it too true
It was too much proof
So I guess I can walk away
Knowing I did my best
But I just need to say
I still love you, and the rest?
Well It was my fairytale
One I saw fading
And it grew stale
And now there's no faking

Do You Really Know Me?

You know I'm a freeze baby
So I'm thinking maybe
You really knew what I was
But then I hear its only because
I told you a million times
Then you followed in their crimes
So how am I to trust you
When I know what you do
You twist me into the powerless
Just with that caress
How am I to believe
Its really me you see
When every other girl is cute
And I'm to stay on mute
Just agree with a nod
And give that ego another prod
So in answer no I'm not coming back
I've already fought off enough attacks

Escape

Constantly calling only to hear a dial tone
No I'm not here and even if I was I'm not alone
You can't stop by to see if my skin is unscarred
There are some lines from you pushing too hard
I don't want to hear your regret
What I really want is to forget
Is it that hard to let me go
Given everything you already know
No I won't be on tonight
And I don't want to be in sight
I want to disappear from you
Maybe it will be easier to forget everything I do
I wake you up with kisses
Talk about being your misses
And it turns out that you weren't happy
You still wanted the untrue fantasy

Should Have

You say you know what went wrong
So you send me lyrics to the same sad song
What should have happened so clearly stated
But thing is you're too jaded
You didn't have to buy me flowers
Or spend hour after hour
Just being near me
You had to make me weak
Before we could be strong
But I guess everything went wrong
So don't think you can sum it up
With some sappy love song
I guess its just another thing you did all wrong

What Went Right

you tell me its done
that all hope is gone
but when I hear that song
I remember not everything went wrong
There were times I was happy
Because you made me
There were times I would cry
Because you didn't ask why
All I wanted was to be wanted
Now all I am is haunted
By all the nights in your arms
All the times you guarded me from harm
All those sweet words
All the avoided hurt
I know you did your best
So forget the rest
But your best didn't include
My own escape from the blue

Dropping Her Guard

Every fiber of her being screamed never again
And she set her focus on not letting them in
As long as no one touched her heart
No one could have the opportunity to tear it apart
If she hid away from the world
She could avoid so much hurt
She never knew her plan would fail
That no matter what evil prevails
She made the mistake of allowing one
And after years all trace of trust is gone
She grew up just to cry herself to sleep
Wondering between love and sanity, which to keep
It wasn't supposed to be this way
It was supposed to be all okay
Slowly she starts to withdraw
Forcing herself to keep moving....as the pain slows her to a crawl

Make Believe

Day to day is a struggle
When waiting for it all to crumble
The smiles and laughs turn fake
The mundane a torture you can't take
You feel like just going away
Find some kind of space
All there is to do is wake up and go
Never letting the true hurt show
A weakness no one can see
Too focused on trying to believe
Every little twisted lie
Just keep the sadness from your eyes
They can't see what isn't there
And then they have no reason to be scared
Now is not the time to let them know,
That you've done everything but go

Severed Bond

He came back to her, too late
His past cruelty sealed their fate
He finally gave what she begged for
Right as she didn't want it anymore
She didn't care that he was ready to change
Their love already felt estranged
She spent years pleading her case
Only to feel easily replaced
After years of feeling like background
Her heart just stopped with no sound
She could see in his eyes the truth
There was no point in further proof
There was no trace of remorse
And finally she knew her life's course

Callous

For every problem, an excuse
To her there was no use
Everything twisted in on her
Until it all became a chaotic blur
She felt herself strain
Under such an incredible weight
And then the inevitable buckle.
At his callous chuckle
He dared mock her pain as silly
They assumed it was her acting dramatically
But the tears and hurt were real
It cut to her core and never healed
And at the sound she came undone
She let go of all that had been clinging on
She finally accepted that the words were wasted
And regardless of all she did, their love was ill-fated

He Thought

He thought he knew her every whim
Her tendency to always give in
He thought she wouldn't notice him pushing
Of the constant judging
Don't do this, or act like that
Every action under attack
He thought she was at fault
His scrutiny never to halt
She begged him to see
To understand she needed to be free
Regardless of what he changed
He could not erase the past strain
He should have seen this coming
When things got overwhelming she had a habit of running

Survive

Just hold tight darling
This tragedy will be scarring
In a way not many will be able to see
And those tears will still glean
The ride is going to be rough
The healing process slow and tough
She just has to hang on tight
The world will go on
And this will be another battle won
It may take time
But eventually she will be fine
Just at this moment her sanity is frayed
And she has a long journey to okay

Hold Tight

She searches for the spark
It was there
Before it all went dark
She screams and it's unfair
No one is present to hear
No one to play witness
So she halts the tears
Hiding deep within distress
They all try to add a little
To her more of a burden
Her sanity whittled
She escapes within herself
To a place of safety
She pulls her heart from the shelf
And holds tight to her last shred of humanity

Broken Dependency

Shattered, she looks up hopelessly
Become someone I can depend on please
He just walks on
The task left undone
Silly girl should have known better
Now to focus on not turning bitter
Time and time again he disappoints her
And she just stares in wonder
How could one claim so much love
And yet not chose her above
And of the silly worldly things
She cringes at the snapping of her heart strings
She believed in a man that failed miserably
No need to live life in misery
She understands now that the time has come to walk away
And hope like hell that soon it will be okay

My Worth

I was worth being enough
I was worth fighting through the bluff
You never understood that side
Always seeing the fun ride
I was worth having a safe place
And not having to hide my face
I deserved to be respected
Not the constant rejection
I deserved to have my man back me
Not be the one to push me off the edge into nothing
But you refused to get that
You refused to take a step back
Now I ran with no hesitation
And you start to give explanations
No longer filled with excuses
For they have out lived their uses

His Cruel Ignorance

He couldn't have possibly meant what he said
Surely it is something he admits he regrets
Sadly that is not the case
And the tears start a trail down her face
He had the nerve to claim ignorance
While destroying their long awaited bliss
There was a time he would have fought
But perhaps that's another thing he forgot
He seems to recall less as time goes on
And she is wondering if it's time to get gone
He put the blame solely on her
And threw her to be consumed by the fire
She fought the odds on him
Swore they would never give in
Then the day finally came
And there was no need to explain
The door closed silently
And her final words "I wish you actually needed me."

Needed You

I allowed myself some weakness
Never thinking you would do this
I depended on you
To be left with no clue
It is highly rare
For me to ask for anyone to care
But you made me expect it
Only to leave me rejected
I needed you to let me crumble
To incoherently mumble
About the unfairness of the world
To scream at the deepest hurt
For once in my life I needed a man
And somehow this is too high a demand

Plastic Smiles

Dutifully she wears the disguise
A fake smile and sparkle in her eyes
Regardless of how she truly feels
She has to make them believe the happy is real
So she steadies her breathing
And pleads her hands to stop shaking
Her tears have been wiped away
Hopefully she looks okay
Inside she shatters daily
But she can't show the crazy
Hidden from others she breaks a thousand times
Knowing each and every crime
They expect life to just continue
But moving becomes a struggle when the day starts anew
She can put on a brave face
But nothing fills the lonely space

Unraveling

He smirks as he watches her tail spin
Her brand of chaos so alluring
She smiles as she start to undo
And the darkness spreads anew
She remembers a far off place
Where they remember the tears that railed her face
She recalls the fire build from within
And giving in to darkest sin
But all he can see is the trace
Of what was her beauty and grace
He finds her losing control
A sign of trying to be whole
He rejoices in her chaos, the darkness
For it was her form of fighting the hopeless

Reconciliation

When it comes down to it
We finally admit the truth
Apart we couldn't bear it
It was a darkness that consumed
We tried to go our separate ways
But yet again true love remains
There is no denying what is there
So its time to repair
We made a vow to love for life
And I never want to stop being your wife
It may take time to succeed
But you always make me believe
From the day we met I have loved you
And I still do, no matter how hard I tried not to

Soulmates

Soulmates should never be apart
For that is what breaks the heart
Love may tarnish and fade
Soulmates is a promise the universe made
There is no inching away
Forever and for always
Once you find that one
Who makes your heart drum
The one who draws you in like a magnet
And you just need to have it
When the distance hurts
Like a searing iron
That's when you know the love is worth
Just a little more fight hun

Pretty Face

They told her she was weak
That her goals were not fitting for a pretty face
To them her appearance meek
But to judge solely on appearance, to her a disgrace
So she fought to prove them wrong
To show that the odds against her meant nothing
To show just how strong
She could be when she wanted something
So she dug deeper
And watched the climb get steeper
Inside and out she just grinned
There was no way this was a battle she would not win
She set her course
And left no time for remorse
In time they would have to see
Why it was never wise to underestimate a pixie

Rebellion

I chose leather instead of lace
and get labeled a disgrace.
Tattoos instead of bows
I'm evil don't you know?
Society has its' norms
and I'm expected to just conform
No one asks my side
or even asks how I survived
I'm covered in labels
and considered out of control
The edge I have is not understood
I'm just labeled as anything but good.
It's ok to have these labels
to make everyone else the fools
I would rather be underestimated
and put up with being unduly hated
than have people truly know me
and only have unending pity
Rough around the edges is only just a mask
but for me it accomplishes my task

Coming Back to Life

With each step she sheds the cloak of self doubt
Finally coming to terms with what she is about
She was not built to bow
Her will just does not know how
The scars have healed, leaving a path of survival
And her eyes open to her soul's revival
The bounce returns to her step
Released from the strain of being "kept"
She has stood in the middle of the storm
Being constantly beaten and torn
She has felt every single lightening bolt
The memory still brings the pain of each jolt
But finally there is but a glimmer
Just a tiny little flicker
And from the storm she emerges
The hope of the glimmer surges
With eyes open she can finally realize
Love does not hurt, loyalty is free
And in the end it's safe to be happy

Life's Hurdles

What happened to the wonder in your face?
What caused the fall from grace?
Shyly she just replies "very slowly"
He could not begin to comprehend the complexity
Slowly every guy showed a true side
Slowly they all chose that was not by hers
Slowly life took her piece by piece
Slowly and surely she grew weak
Then a reprieve, a slight relief
Out of the wreckage came her forever
And she dared to dream of a future
Slowly life again turned upside down
Slowly it swallowed her whole
Slowly she relearned the comfort of numb
How to silently go emotionally dumb
At every hill she conquered there was a mountain
Life fated her to have to fight to win
So she closed herself off from emotion
From hoping and dreaming, or demanding devotion
She set her path through the jagged landscape
And ignored the pain of any cuts or scrapes
She learned not to shatter at any cost
Because then all dignity is lost
That's what he said after all
People will pity her and delight at her fall
So though hollow, she stands staring blankly at the next hurdle

Keep Silent

Don't ask, don't tell
She knew that rule so well
She knew to keep silent
Just ignore the violent
In time it would be done
And she could do her best to move on
For now its clothes covering bruises
And hoping like hell she doesn't lose it
She holds on tight
And tries to win the fight
One day she will be able to stand tall
Watching their abrupt downfall
For now she wails silently
Refusing to beg or plead

Unreachable

He used to count the tears
And shelter from the fears
He used to pay attention
His love never to question
She knew he would always be there
Even when she was uncontrollably scared
That's the role he always played
Until the new him came to stay
The one who ignored the hurt
And drug her morals through the dirt
She couldn't get a passing glance
He held a guarded stance
She pleaded and begged
For him not to forget
But just like that his love was gone
And in its place a heart of stone
No matter how hard she tried, she could not reach him
And she knew it was time to finally give in

Stale

He couldn't bring himself to ask
Who would want to reveal under the mask
Who knows what he would find, pain?
God forbid he found her disdain
That would be his undoing
Or maybe she is unraveling
But he dares not question
And she doesn't bother to mention
There is a mystery causing a gap
And finally she lays it all in his lap
She felt lost in his world
And she could no longer ignore her hurt
She felt slightly caged
And extremely enraged
There was no saving their fairytale
It had long since grown stale

Breaking Ties

Day to day is a struggle
When waiting for it all to crumble
The smiles and laughs turn fake
The mundane a torture you can't take
You feel like just going away
Find some kind of space
All there is to do is wake up and go
Never letting the true hurt show
A weakness no one can see
Too focused on trying to believe
Every little twisted lie
Just keep the sadness from your eyes
They can't see what isn't there
And then they have no reason to be scared
Now is not the time to let them know
That you've done everything but go

Estranged

He came back to her, too late
His past cruelty sealed their fate
He finally gave what she begged for
Right as she didn't want it anymore
She didn't care that he was ready to change
Their love already felt estranged
She spent years pleading her case
Only to feel easily replaced
After years of feeling like background
Her heart just stopped with no sound
She could see in his eyes the truth
There was no point in further proof
There was no trace of remorse
And finally she knew her life's course

Keep Moving

Every fiber of her being screamed never again
And she set her focus on not letting them in
As long as no one touched her heart
\no one could have the opportunity to tear it apart
If she hid away from the world
She could avoid so much hurt
She never knew her plan would fail
That no matter what evil prevails
She made the mistake of allowing one
And after years all trace of trust is gone
She grew up just to cry herself to sleep
Wondering between love and sanity, which to keep
It wasn't supposed to be this way
It was supposed to be all okay
Slowly she starts to withdraw
Forcing herself to keep moving…..as the pain slows her to a crawl

Ill-Fated Love

For every problem, an excuse
To her there was no use
Everything twisted in on her
Until it all became a chaotic blur
She felt herself strain
Under such an incredible weight
And then the inevitable weight
And then the inevitable buckle
At his callous chuckle
He dared mock her pain as silly
They assumed it was her acting dramatically
But the tears and hurt were real
It cut to her core and never healed
And at that sound she came undone
She let go of all that had been clinging on
She finally accepted that the words were wasted
And regardless of all she did, their love was ill-fated

Second Chance

This smile won't fade
He brought out the happy place
He made her feel worthy
Never rushed or in a hurry
They could sit in silence peacefully
Who knew she could be this happy?
His arms felt like security
He quickly made quiet all her worries
He pushed her limits with tenderness
To the point she craved his caress
For too long she felt like slipping away
Now she just hopes she can stay
A sweet and fresh beginning
Another chance at a happy ending

Security

He made sleep safe
And her heart quake
The night terrors vanished with ease
And it was relieving to be so pleased
She heard her giggle again
And she couldn't hold it in
He touched a part of her left dormant
And now the hope runs rampant
She reminds herself to slow down
But hr heart beats so loud
Her smile seems brighter and more real
He gave her something she could feel
The doubt is still there
But with each passing day it becomes less of a scare

The Rescue

Slowly he gives her more
And she can peak through the door
She got a glimpse of his pride
A genuine smile he couldn't hide
And in that moment she fell
Her heart wanted to hear everything he could tell
The silly stories that made him cringe
The tragic ones that made his heart twitch
She wanted to know this man like no other
She just hoped he could want her
In his eyes she saw the need
But his warning she attempted to heed
But his smile pulled her in
And her heart and mind were racing
He had no clue the parts he had awakened
Or how her world was shaken
One day he may get to see
How he rescued the pixie

Unbroken

She remembered her strength over the years
All of the overcome tears
She reminded herself she was better than this
That she could find true bliss
She thought of everything she got through
She picked herself back up
And remembered she could be tough
There is a fire within her
And no one could stop her gaining power
Shortly after the greatest fall
She finally realized she wasn't broken after all

Barely Existing

She knew better than to hope anymore
To expect it all to be an adventure
She got used to the day to day
Knowing this was the price she paid
For she wasn't like the rest
She had finally broken under the test
When they pushed and prodded
She felt all but forgotten
They never questioned what she wishes
They just chalked it up to excuses
Until slowly she was drained
Only a ragged shell remained
She didn't need to enjoy the day
Her only duty was to obey
So she dared not to hope
As she barely grasped the end of her rope

Memories

They didn't get to see
Not even a glimpse of her suffering
For too long she held it in
And now it is as if it's stuck there, frozen
If she dared to show
She knew most would choose to go
So silently she sits in the background
Always just kind of around
Until someone notices her silence
And she pretends to be in her own violence
A simple proof of the past
A memory she cannot outlast

The Mocking Sun

The sun rose relentlessly, mocking
It erased the night before like it meant nothing
The distance just kept stretching further
And the ache felt was beyond pure
Resistance was the biggest obstacle
As the heart begged to be full
If only temporary the ache would stop
but that was not even close to the list's top
First was the agony to cross
And hope against all not to be lost
Then there was the numbness that follows
Leaving most empty, hollow
At least there is a sign of being content
Not immediate but growing less and less distant
It will last but a second in the cycle
As the curiosity of the new sets in and spirals
Once again the hope emerges
And once again the mocking sun emerges

Never Slip

She hid right under the surface
Never deceiving on purpose
But they all took out of context
The many times she failed their test
They told her the act was appalling
Never understanding the pain calling
Of course she acted numb
For bitterness burned her tongue
If allowed to slip there would be no going back
And she just knew they couldn't take the attack
Who would want to know that she was broken
Had given up on everything, including hopin'
There is but a shell left
And inside all the pain is kept
Hidden from everyone
Swearing to never come undone

Running

He thought he knew her every whim
Her tendency to always give in
He thought she wouldn't notice him pushing
Of the constant judging
Don't do this, or act like that
Every action under attack
He thought she was at fault
His scrutiny never to halt
She begged him to see
To understand she needed to be free
Regardless of what he changed
He could not erase the past strain
He should have seen this coming
When things get overwhelming she had a habit of running

The Story

When she tells the story they gasp
Who is she to attack
The man he makes himself out to be
But that is not the man she got to see
She saw his anger and contempt
She saw his daily regret
The way he pushed her to the edge
And never hesitated to continue to nudge
The way his words burned like fire
And yet he always claimed his desire
He wore a convincing mask
And always claimed to take it back
The cycle never stopped
Until her heart suddenly popped
With one last statement it all halted
Suddenly she couldn't take being insulted
So she chose to break the silence
And she walked away from all the mental violence

Very Slowly

What happened to the wonder in your face?
What caused the fall from grace?
Shyly she just replies "very slowly"
He could not begin to comprehend the complexity
Slowly every guy showed a true side
Slowly they all chose that was not by hers
Slowly life took her piece by piece
Slowly and surely she grew weak
Then a reprieve, a slight relief
Out of the wreckage came her forever
And she dared to dream of a future
Slowly life again turned upside down
Slowly it swallowed her whole
Slowly she relearned the comfort of numb
How to silently go emotionally dumb
At every hill she conquered, there was a mountain
Life fated her to have to fight to win
So she closed herself off from emotion
From hoping and dreaming, or demanding devotion
She set her path through the jagged landscape
And ignored the pain of any cuts or scrapes
She learned not to shatter at any cost
Because then all dignity is lost
That's what he said after all
People will pity her and delight at her fall
So though hollow, she stands staring blankly at the next hurdle

Abandoned

She never asked more than her worth
She knew better than to stray from the course
She asked for loyalty
Screw being royalty
She wanted for once to be a priority
To be a piece to his clarity
Instead he used her body and mind
Fully intending to leave a shell behind
Of the girl he once knew
That only asked the love to be true
He refused to give her that
And all of her hope fell flat
She picked the pieces up one by one
Reveling in what he had done
He took a beauty rare and pure
And twisted it to her own torture
By the end she questioned her core
And that's when he finally chose to leave her

Damage Control

There is beauty in her
Far deeper than the skin
Filled with fire
Mixed with the sweetest sins
She mastered the art of deception
And found little connection
The outside world a blur
Leaving much to conquer
The fear of rejection
The sting of deception
The pain of feeling alone
The terror of facing things on her own
They all said it would take time
But after all the years she is far from fine
So she fakes it as best she can
And hopes no one forces her hand
Her false bravado starts to fade
And they realize she has been stunted in the shade
They attempt to fix the broken
But the wounds are excessive and open
So they patch her up
And she resumes her role of being tough

Path of Survival

I will never forget
Your lack of regret
The way you placed blame
And left me less than sane
I'm reminded of a struggle
No one saw me have
The way even the slightest mumble
Felt like a vicious attack
They saw a smile made of plastic
Kindness stretched like elastic
They saw what they wanted
And ignored the fact I was haunted
So I picked up the pieces
And gave no reasons
I wiped the scalding tears
While facing down the fears
I walked on with purpose
Reminding myself I didn't deserve this
The pain faded, the tears stopped, and the scream became inaudible
All on the path of survival

His Inner Guilt

He couldn't bring himself to ask
Who would want to reveal under the mask
Who knows what he would find, pain?
God forbid he found her disdain
That would be his undoing
Or maybe she is unraveling
But he dares not question
And she doesn't bother to mention
There is a mystery causing a gap
And finally she lays it all in his lap
She felt lost in his world
And she could no longer ignore the hurt
She felt slightly caged
And extremely enraged
There was no saving their fairytale
It had long since grown stale

Written Poison

As ink leaves pen
The poison leaves her head
She attempts to remember
That things get better
The pain finally stopped
But she never forgot
His taunting smile
Made her numb after a while
His bellowing voice
Had taken her choice
She reserved her right to let go
To just learn how to float
He could not take that from her
No matter how he must suffer
She keeps this all in her head
As she contemplates the end

Play Your Role

They told her she was weak
That her goals were not fitting for a pretty face
To them her appearance meek
But to judge solely on appearance, to her a disgrace
So she fought to prove them wrong
To show that the odds against her meant nothing
To show just how strong
She could be when she wanted nothing
So she dug deeper
And watched the climb get steeper
Inside and out she just grinned
There was no way this was a battle she couldn't win
She set her course
And left no time for remorse
In time they would have to see
Why it was never wise to underestimate a pixie

The Cost of Living

There is beauty in her
For deeper than skin
Filled with fire
Mixed with the sweetest sin
She mastered the art of deception
And found little connection
The outside world a blur
Leaving much to conquer
The fear of rejection
The sting of deception
The pain of feeling alone
The terror of facing things on her own
They all said it would take time
But after all the years she is far from fine
So she fakes it as best she can
And hopes no one forces her hand
Her fake bravado starts to fade
And they realize she has been stunted in the shade
They attempt to fix the broken
But the wounds are too extensive, and open
So they patch her up
And she resumes the role of being tough

Downfall

The first time he bought her flowers
And they sat talking for hours
He swore never again
So she let him right back in
The second time he swore she provoked him
She knew how much he hated that sarcastic grin
He yelled so loud she dutifully apologized
While steadily averting her eyes
The 107th time, well she obviously asked for it
She knew her place and just wouldn't stay put
If she just minded his rules
His temper would cool
The last time she didn't even fight back
So calmly accepting his attack
She asked for it, deserved it, knew better, but couldn't learn
His only choice was to beat it into her
Then finally she took it all in, like a tidal wave of clarity
She saw for once his complete depravity
And breaking all rules, she allowed herself to be once again free

Emotional Exhaustion

If you knew the scars still bleed
Would that be enough to make you believe
That maybe, just maybe, it truly cut that deep
That maybe it is more than just memories
The sleepless nights may be explained
But so far she has felt too ashamed
How does an unbreakable woman admit
She was still too weak and accepted it
That she allowed so much hate to be poured into her
She isn't convinced it will ever be truly over
From now on she may only see her flaws
The ones he pointed out "just because"
Her voice may always be quiet
Her mind in a constant riot
The true hope is the torment will end
But she is far too tired to pretend

Her Purpose

Blindly giving love that will never be returned
She has learned how to easily accept the hurt
Acting as the saving grace
Never showing anguish on her face
Accepting the full weight of others' decisions
For the sake of staying true to a mission
To be the slight glimmer of hope
The one to keep it all afloat
Never daring to crack under the pressure
Her duty is to always reassure
Until all demons are finally put to rest
This shall be her path, her test

Justifications

Nothing she ever did was right
He will say, justifying every fight
She didn't clean often enough
Dealing with her "laziness" was tough
She didn't dress up the right way
That kind of shit would ruin his whole day
She asked from him far too much
Yet dared to flinch at his touch
Every step she took was wrong
Why couldn't she go along to get along
He will claim absolutely no fault
As he continues his oh so justified assault

Make Use

Make sense of the chaos
Before all hope is lost
Make use of the time
Before losing your mind
Make use of the beauty in life
For it passes quickly by
Make use of the pain
For the hurt will never stay the same
Make use of the sorrow
Turn it into a fight for tomorrow
Make use of the misery
Go ahead and let it leave you gritty
Just please make use of it all
Before it makes use of you and you learn only to crawl

Manipulations

Sadly the man I thought cared
Has been replaced by one who leaves me scared
I see all the contempt he holds in his heart
And it is more than enough to tear me completely apart
Years of giving my absolute all
Has set me up for the harshest fall
His unhappiness much more than haunting
The list of my failures beyond daunting
They told me to be his peace
Did they know that meant being weak?
When they demanded such complex tasks
Did they know one slip was instant attack?
If they did would it even have mattered?
Or would the result still be the same, me being battered?

Never Knew

If life slowed for a mere moment
Would it be enough to help her forget
The way his sweetness quickly faded
And his love turned wicked
How one misstep
Would lead to days of regret
He stopped controlling his rage
Throwing tantrums, forgetting his age
Patiently she waited
For his contempt to be sated
Instead it grew and grew
Until one day he became a man she never knew

New Haven

It was understood that she fought a war
He could see it in her armor
The walls she built thick and high
Maybe one day he would dare to ask why
The way loud noises made her quickly assess
And though she tried there would be no rest
Not one piece of her felt truly safe
So she wandered place to place
Hoping to find a world all her own
One where its safe to be alone
One removed completely from him
Her biggest regret was ever letting him in

Self-Sacrifice

Years of being completely alone, even in the biggest crowds
She never imagined silence could be so loud
That having a partner could get so lonely
Enough to leave her wondering if she'd ever be seen
Questions flow rapid fire through her mind
Was it all just an act, was she truly that blind
Were the signs always there
And she just refused to care
What made her believe she could erase the evil within
To push with such blind optimism
Swallowing down all his harsh criticisms
To start believing so many lies about herself
From a man who only offered her hell

Lonely

When the voices fade
And all is back in place
Can you enjoy the empty
Or is it a new tragedy
Are you so lost in the crowd
That only peace can be found in the loud
In the beautiful forced smiles
And the falsehood of running wild
Sitting still must be a personal hell
One you cannot dare tell
For the shame comes in being weak
In admitting such a pathetic need

Push Through

She faced it all alone
Never finding he heart's home
Swearing she could handle it all
Refusing to admit how hard she could fall
She dusted off all the misery
To prove she didn't feel the lonely
To show she didn't feel the lonely
To show she was always tough
Trained from a young age to get back up
Life was pure tragedy
But she couldn't live on her knees
So no one saw the tired in her eyes
And they blindly bought into all the tough girl lies
And life numbly went on
Because she has no choice but be strong

Pixie

From a deep, cold sleep the pixie awakens
She opens her star filled eyes
Unravels her elegant, yet scarred wings
Feeling the fire build within, she smirks
There is power within her unmatched
There is a freedom only she can provide
Doubting her survival is beyond ignorance
She starts to take strides in this fight
She moves closer to the edge he taught her to fear
The one he claimed would be her undoing
The one he used to keep her kept
She reaches the edge and dives no hesitation
Suddenly soaring more free than she ever dared
Pixie finally accepts being whole. Body, mind and soul

Waking Pixie

From a deep, cold sleep the pixie awakens
She opens her star filled eyes
Unravels her elegant, yet scarred wings
Feeling the fire building within she smirks
There is power within her unmatched
There is a freedom only she can provide
Doubting her survival is beyond ignorance
She starts to take strides in this fight
She moves closer to the edge he taught her to fear
The one he claimed would be her undoing
The one he used to keep her kept
She reaches the edge and dives no hesitation
Suddenly soaring more free than she ever dared
Pixie finally accepts being whole. Body, mind and soul

Pretty Little Pets

Pretty little pets don't ever talk back
Obedience means unquestioning silence
Pretty little pets are never too tired
Their role forever servitude
Pretty little pets make a point to stay pretty
No excuses for poor appearance
Remember the role
Pretty little pets never ask for themselves
It was never about them in the first place
Pretty little pets swallow the shame
They freely accept the blame
Pretty little pets live only to say yes
Never showing true signs of distress
Pretty little pets are only a fantasy
One made for a weak man incapable of truly loving
Pretty little pets rebel
Finally escaping a custom built hell

Internal Inferno

Little flashes, sparks really, kindle the fire
The one that consumes all peace within her
Stoked by hateful thought processes
Turned inward screaming she is worthless
It burns red hot as it mocks
False confidence devoured when she forgot
This path means scalding truth
Leaving only rubble as proof
The fortress she once was
Demolished by his anger, just because
Crawling from an immense inferno
That no amount of distance will let her go
These flickers just at her heels
Swallowing her shadow, reminding her to feel
Feel useless, weak, powerless, lost in a dark oasis
Stranded from kindness, feeling love as absolute drought
Rebuild, tear down. Rebuild, tear down. Demolish
That is why deeply having peace is her only wish

Inner Strength

Know your true worth
Never let them control the hurt
Fight like hell and take some names
Never hide yourself in shame
Remove the comfort of self doubt
Find just one thing to have strength about
The pain will end if you so wish
Just allow yourself a taste of bliss
Nothing in life has a guarantee
You have to force yourself to believe
Believe in the power within
Never back down from a sadistic grin
Strength is a shield no one can break
And life is built on the chances you take
Living freely is a battle you fight daily
One you can lose if allowed to be shaken

Silence

They ask how she kept silent
How she hid his violent
Matching shades became a career
Much like her swallowing fear
Flinching was just second nature
Pretend as though nothing phased her
Each step checked, calculated, measured
For years convinced she was only hated
A deeply built belief
One with no true relief
She was nothing more than a burden
So she did her best to stay hidden
Speak softly, smile often
Do all she could to avoid a coffin
Taught this was the love she deserved
She unquestioningly served
Her sick and twisted master
Feeling her soul fade faster and faster
Her silence easily bought
With the fear of if she actually fought

Break Beautifully

Oh darling if you truly need it to be
Can you please at least break beautifully?
Don't let the world strip you away
Do not allow them to enforce your dismay
Crumble into a pile that is managed
Seem as far from damaged
Do not allow the world to crush your spirit
Demand that with every step they feel it
Losing yourself would be a great injustice
Please do not allow anyone that power over this
They do not deserve that right over you
No one is permitted to leave you completely unglued
So hold it all together for your own sake
Hold it together, and beautifully break
Into a million pieces and beyond
And then repair the damage and peacefully move on

Chemistry

Craving your touch with every glimpse
Knowing there is no moment I want to miss
The feel of your skin under my fingers
Tempting myself to allow them to linger
To trace a trail to all that seems forbidden
Exploring in ways that leave nothing hidden
To bring, with a simple touch, an uncontrolled quake
To have the power to reach a soul and gently shake
The need for the taste of your lips possessing mine
The electric energy as bodies intertwine
My mind wandering through all the sweet torment
All the thoughts making clear their intent
The things I hold back gleefully taunt me
Reminding how badly my need for you is growing
My sweet chaos filled man in all his glory
Let me show you just how wild my chaos can be

Daily Serving

They ask why she is so tough
But the truth is just too rough
How can she reveal all the scars
Without allowing it to go too far
There was a time there was her honor
All the things life attempted to steal from her
The moments she forced herself to reclaim
For once refusing to hold all of the blame
Explaining how manipulation became breakfast
And there was no escape from it
Rage the best lunch in town
And "Jesus, you're pretty when you scowl."
She ended her nights wrapped in a thick layer of shame
Knowing she invited every moment of his game
Yet reminding herself daily it is within him
And sometimes the best defense was to just give in

Eye of The Storm

Cry, scream, beg, whimper, fight
Let the world learn your might
Tear apart all that once was
If for nothing more than because
Don't plan an explanation unearned
Take the time to see who is willing to learn
Who will stand in the center of your storm
If for nothing more than to keep you warm
No soul could bear the weight of your hell
Don't expect any rescue, don't bother to tell
The story is full of heartbreak
That most only accept when faked
The real life stories are too shameful
Must pretend you weren't that controlled
But once that one withstands the storm by your side
Well then my dear understand the worth in taking it in stride
Give your all and then some
For that dedication is one far too unsung

104

Redefinition

To get lost in absolute peace
To know that is what will end his feast
Being hidden all these years in the shadows
Instead of freely frolicking in meadows
Things took a turn
And the bitter taste still holds a burn
To look back is an ache she no longer craves
Suddenly she finds a will to survive with grace
Dancing on the right side of wrong
Knowing there is no limit to her strong
Stumbling is human, crumbling to be expected
The path to this point cruel, her soul rejected
No sweet girl don't do that, follow the rules
Only to finally realize obedience invited the cruel
So she puts down the burden of perfection
And in her freedom welcomes rejection
Seeing for once that rejection measures their worth
Living how she wishes is all that defines her

Reject Society

No one knew what her shy kept hidden
Exactly what society has told her is forbidden
What kind of person loves freely
What kind of person chooses grace daily
Who said your heart didn't need charred
So many expect you to be beaten down
Please be just another mindless clown
It shocks them to see you take a stand
To make it clear you have this all in your hand
That power landed back into your lap
And for once you cling to the right to not take crap
How unfortunate society tries to deny the process
Of someone overcoming their own mess

Secret Mission

When she raised her voice, he laughed
His cruelty never held back
Speak when spoken to darling
Heed every clear warning
Do not step out of line
Know your place during this time
Allow him his foolish pride
Let it swallow him whole and subside
His faults do not have to bleed into you
There is a chance to walk away and start anew
The freedom she can obtain
Is one hardly contained
Watch her unravel neatly
Rebel ever so discreetly
And when all is said and done
Understand there is no battle that cannot be won

Stand Down

They ask without truly wanting to know
They truly wish you would just let go
Take that little flash of hope and smother it
That tiny flicker of conviction needs to turn to forfeit
How dare you face down your fears
How dare you continue to challenge your peers
This life was not meant to be lived self governed
Society demands that by now all must have learned
How to speak and move properly
How to accept their fate unquestioning
Fit the role perfectly assigned to them
Do not dare push beyond what you were given
How dare you expect more from life
Fighting the destiny of your personally assigned strife
Know your place is the rule to the game
And if you dare speak different it ends all the same

Sweet Girl

Remember to dream sweet girl
Remember to smile and shock the world
Remember there is an inferno inside you
One not a soul can undo
The way it shatters only to mend
How the cracks show as you continue to bend
The strength to mold to life's circumstance
Never backing down or changing your stance
Life was cruel and highly unfair
Just remember that beautiful flare
The one that took word into action
Turned a drop of lust into raging passion
Only you hold all of that power
Making the world yours to devour
Just don't forget to remember sweet girl
You are forever the ruler of your world

The Act

There were times she will never recall
Things done that were just too much
Remembering would surely be her downfall
None registered more than a tender touch
With an audience he danced elegantly
Behind closed doors he shied no beating
He swore they would never buy her version
Simply through his sick coercion
Making it seem there was no true escape
And she had forever decided her fate
Freedom just an impossible leap
That she dare not feat
One day she always proclaimed
Until finally that one day came
Shaken to her core she stopped fighting
And the power of that simple gesture, frightening

The Cost

The bruises faded faster than the pain
The pieces she lost could not be regained
That innocence forever lost
He never understood the true cost
He believed she would eventually rebound
And finally be able to get off the ground
Problem was his fists seemed too powerful
The pain just took its toll
He thought a spirit like hers was resilient
But turns out sometimes it just isn't
Some of the pain cannot be escaped
And no kindness can begin to leave it erased
She wonders if this knowledge would have stopped him
As she regrets the moments she let him in
There is no shame in what the world has done
But she will never see that as she holds on
Life will leave you broken and confused
But she took it another step, allowing herself to be used

The Reaction

He didn't expect her to finally react
Far too comfortable with her accepting the attack
It was her fault at all times
How could she ever question the grime
The way she was used and abused
Should have been her first clue
He never truly saw her worth
Just focused on dragging her through the dirt
He never imagined she would rediscover her fight
That one day she would take off in beautiful flight
That no one could keep her soul caged
It only took unleashing the saved rage
The growl he never saw coming
As he failed to outrun it
After allowing all to break loose
She finally admits this is what he decided to choose
A life without her, all that sparkled and was pure
He threw it all away the moment he attempted to control her

Tiny Dancer

The girl I was danced without care
She didn't realize it was a hidden dare
The girl I was loved without limit
She never thought anyone would abuse it
The girl I was never flinched at a simple voice
She thought she would always have a choice
The girl I was held no bitterness or shame
She had yet to even learn his name
The girl I was got swept up in a false fairytale
She never saw the inevitable fail
The girl I was gave it her absolute all
She quickly learned his order was just too tall
So the woman I am now took the steps needed
Regardless if the process stayed heated
The woman I am now gathers her strength calmly
Knowing without a doubt the storm is coming
The woman I am now is ready to dance in the rain
And revel in all the glorious, freeing pain

Victory

Take a deep breath and just be
Live just a moment without animosity
Allow the bitterness to pass through you
Understand letting go is fool proof
There is no benefit to holding onto the anger
All that would do is swallow her
So understand why she chooses this path
One in which she forgets to look back
The past holds nothing more than lessons
Just bundled up, fucked up messes
Ones she has already overcome
So now she realizes the battle is won
No more shots being fired
She can finally rest, retired
She takes that final deep breathe of clarity
Knowing without a doubt survival is a rarity

Impossible Demands

The last thing she expected was abandonment
How after all that she gave could he just drop it
She lay awake wondering where she went wrong
Just what made their love fall short of strong
Seriously considering it was all her fault
If only she wasn't so difficult
Knowing that her best was never enough
Nothing truly earned her his love
Once that was clear she settled more
She realized there was nothing worth fighting for
Long before she finally gave in
He made it impossible to win
His terms ever changing
His demands unrelenting
So while abandonment was last on her mind
She accepts he had never been so kind

Cruel Intent

The dream he promised faded fast
The lies he told couldn't last
For underneath the surface was cruelty
A piece of him, he didn't want her to see
But the veil lifted one fateful day
And her heart knew not to stay
So empty inside she stuck by his side
Chanting she committed to this ride
She never knew any better
She wanted to live, he wouldn't let her
The pain she did her best to conceal
Just for a moment acting like it wasn't real
No that mark wasn't from him
He wouldn't dare blemish her skin
He wouldn't dare hit a woman
That is why she can't truly be broken
He threw words like daggers
And wondered why she staggered
The mystery still left unsolved
As she starts to dissolve
Everyone told her actions speak louder than words
And with that she ended her own hurt

Justice Denied

They toss blame on her completely
None willing to admit his insanity
How each day she was worthless
And each night still required to caress
His oh so fragile male pride
And they all just watched from the side
No one dared to step in
And her compliance more than a given
If anyone questioned it
None felt the need to actually commit
To standing their ground for her
Just let her live in horror
Yet the day she finally cut ties
All that horror she lived was "lies"
No one ever saw the abuse
She thought what was the use
Why waster her breathe
On those proven useless

Recovery

Silently she screams
Always nightmares, never dreams
Her heart scarred from wars lost
No one will ever know the true cost
The nights alone hating herself
The complete lack of any help
The man she vowed her life to
Acting as though she was just a tool
Using her body as a weapon
The pain will never lessen
Instead she has to swallow it down
In the hopes she will one day wear that crown
The one made of pure victory
From finally fighting to be free
One day she will finally heal
And be able to finally learn to feel
Feeling whole and strong for no one else
But the wonderful woman she is, only herself

Anxiety

The dread fills her instantly
The need for self loathing
It tell her nothing will work out
It shrouds every move in complete doubt
Screaming so only she can hear
Criticizing all she holds dear
How could she ever be more
Just accept the absolute mediocre
That was all she was ever worth
No end to the overbearing hurt
Daily chanting failure into her every move
As she dutifully followed the cues
No one else saw the broken side
In her mind it chose to hide
Until it had her alone once again
Making it clear she would never win
No matter what the outside saw
It claimed all peace and left her raw
They just cannot comprehend why she seems so tortured
But this anxiety shit will never release her

Inner Torment

It came on suddenly at too early a stage
One day happy, the next full of pure rage
The reflection twisted to an ugliness
There was no way for her to repress
The confidence nothing more than faked
It was all part of the perfect play
The anger wouldn't allow a misstep
That was a mistake she could not forget
Stupid girl why did you stumble
Silly girl be nothing but humble
Her mind would not allow her to be whole
It demanded she fall deeper in the hole
Standing up was never an option
Doubting herself more than often
The twists in her mind treacherous
How could she ever attempt to escape this
The hatred was deeply ingrained
It knew her by name
Nothing satisfied its thirst
Except for her eternal hurt

Internal Doom

Eyes open, no peace
Eyes closed, still no release
Regardless of her need for a break
There was always more punishment to take
Don't dare speak out
She had to accept all self doubt
The way her mind mocked
Reminding her she is easily forgot
No one will notice her insignificance
How could she ask for more than this
Her worth ingrained deep within
Never worth investing in
Her duty was to be the healer
As her mind slowly broke her
The hope always being it would be appeased
That eventually it just might leave
But that hope was quickly shattered
As it made clear her actions never mattered
Nothing she could ever do
Would give her freedom from the internal doom

Self-Loathing

Long ago she was so carefree
There was no limit on her happy
Then little thoughts crept in
Reminding her of every presumed sin
She didn't smile enough
She acted far too tough
The walls started to inch closer
There is no option of closure
How could that ever be
With these demons being so controlling
Forgiving herself became impossible
All she could see was a foolish girl
She allowed the abuse
She must have begged to be used
The demons mocked her constantly
To the point she lost her sanity
Nothing she ever did could go right
Living daily in such intense fright
She deserved every internal insult
It screamed everything is her fault
No one would convince her otherwise
For her demons were just too wise

The Monster

The monster whispered sweetly in her ear
Repeating all she was expected to fear
Her worth barely measurable
Her presence far from pleasurable
Everyone saw her as a chore
The monster hired a choir
To sing her lullabies
And fill her head with lies
No one will love you it taunts
Everyone will leave it flaunts
The empty spaces that once were
The monster starts to stir
It mocks her daily
Reminding her of the short comings
The monster never rests
Putting her sanity to the test
All she wants is to finally silence
The onslaught of mental violence

Unique Charisma

Suddenly she realized she held a very unique charisma
Shining like the brightest star in the blackest night
Acting as a beacon of hope for the lost souls
Guiding them through their journey of turmoil
Whether being permitted to stay or pass through
People gravitated to her pure soul
And as long as she allowed it to flow freely
All could see her absolute beauty
This beauty did not lay within her eyes, lips, or face
There was no sign of it in her curves
This beauty was buried deep inside her
In such a way no one was capable of dousing it
There was no beating it down, snuffing it out
The world had tried so hard to bury her in bitterness
But she came out the other side even more flawless
The strength she gained was so intense
She could not hide her own power from others
They caught glimpses of the light, and wondered at the glow
She gave a love and acceptance completely unknown
The way she held out her hand towards the next one,
Without care, worry, or reluctance
For some was the refreshing break their tattered souls needed
And supplying that beauty to the world left her whole, completed

Black Abyss

How dare she attempt to claim strength
There was so much doubt in her presence
"When will thus end, when will it crash?"
Her mind spread doom like a rash
There is no point in fighting the inevitable
This was the internal dialogue she lived through
She knew better, she knew better…..fuck she knew better
This was the cycle out to get her
Regardless of the progress made
She only saw her countless mistakes
She was told not to be so harsh
But onward her mind would march
Into the absolute black abyss
There was no escaping this
Her new hope was to train her mind
To once and for all be kind
To give up the need to live in terror
To constantly replay all past horror
Is she could possibly accomplish this task
Maybe her sanity she could take back

Manic

There were days the weight wouldn't lift
In which the day was less than a gift
Days she had to focus her breathing
And hide her absolute breaking
Waking in a pure panic
Her thoughts beyond manic
Between the list of tasks and flaws
Not once did the torment halt
So she would bury herself in blank sleep
And hope against all odds her peace would keep
The cycle continued endlessly
There was no way to obtain true release
At times the demons were more controlled
The she almost felt capable
Yet this was short lived
The demons had too much criticism to give
Every accomplishment just not enough
And the downward spiral was tough
No matter what merit the outside saw in her
The inner voice was cruelly critical

Fake Connection

Blind trust plain dangerous
Always better to be cautious
No one truly worth that place
Every deal just blowing up in their face
Giving out far more than taken
Kindness sadly mistaken
Ties quickly unraveling
Loyalty suddenly wavering
None understand the true limit
There are just some things you cannot forfeit
There is no price on integrity
There is no bargain for the fire in me
Some may claim they bought in
Only a few were truly trusted
The rest were fed a false bravado
Then distance to the let go
Given a script they would swallow
None learning it was all hollow
You only see what I choose
Playing me is a game you'll always lose

New Found Rebellion

Taking strides to a new life
One without limits of daily strife
When it starts to take hold
There is no longer a lack of control
This re building will be breathtaking
Leaving doubters shaken
If ever there was a time for remorse
Those against her to change their course
Deciding finally do as she pleases
Things that her mind always teased
What if she followed her own path
What if she stopped looking back
The options were endless
All she gave up was powerless
No hesitation left in her soul
Enough bravery to just let go
To finally see the role she played
Simply by being so well behaved
So she started to find ways to rebel
Built herself a sweeter version of hell
No longer cowering in a corner
Once and for all, she is the only one who owns her

Partners In Crime

The process was one not many took on
It was impossible to move along
So many chances caught in his eyes
In him her peace lies
The way his happy makes her smile
Loving every moment of her wild
He notices what others ignored
Leaving her completely floored
He swore he refused to fall
But could not resist her loving call
Amazed by her unwavering patience
Her ability to offer pure acceptance
\no longer questioning every I love you
All the while providing her with security
A long ago forgotten bit of peace
Letting her know she has a partner in him
And that it is safe to give in
Neither truly understanding the magic they held together
Just being shown there is no storm they cannot weather
In their simplicity they found a home
A chance to finally rebuild without the need to be alone

Resistance

She asked to be loved simply
To make a life built on happy
The were no conditions listed
His presence leaving her gifted
The way they fit something to behold
A bond purely impenetrable
Others attempted to place doubt
But she knew this was her turnabout
Her way to learn about partnership
To be allowed to finally not be the only one handling it
This mixture was one meant to last
A reason to finally forgive her past
It left her scarred enough to have the courage
To go for what she wanted, and watch it flourish
The man underneath all she had hoped for
Acting for her heart like a cure
Loving him came up unexpected
A hope long since rejected
By chance she persisted through his fear
Simply telling him "I'll be here."
Until the day it became too much to deny
They found exactly what love was in life

Slow Progress

Tell me again who I should be
Enforce the vision of timid and weak
Go ahead remind me of my role
You assume this world took a toll
I know what is expected
But conformity is easily rejected
I refuse to play that game
To be the one hidden in shame
The world may have meant to take me there
To leave me so much more than bare
But the fight must continue
The heart must always be true
Allowing it all to flow through her
Taking the lesson, and stopping to suffer
Then picking up her pride once again
And forcing herself to move on
Keep that marvelous heart
Do not allow the world to take her art
You may see her as purely tortured
But there is a force within her
One she chooses to use constantly
To finally put forth progress daily

Unexpected Love

Inching closer to a connection to her
Feeling the tug of a unique allure
The battle to stay disconnected
A thought long since rejected
The safety offered completely unmatched
A true definition of a catch
All that he was sure he did not want
Soon becoming points he gladly flaunts
A loving woman with no limitations
A pure trust with no hesitation
All he believed unobtainable
She was surprisingly capable
All the warnings he gave
Where nothing against the peace she made
Settling a wandering soul
Reminding daily he was beautiful
No need for change or sacrifice
Only a need to enjoy life
No pressure or need to answer to
The kind of love neither knew
So worth every moment they shared
Teaching each other how to once again care

Unstoppable

How do you put terms to the undefinable
The things that seem truly impossible
Is there a way to describe the feeling
Beyond saying it is amazing
Would the fates laugh at such a simple statement
As if the creativity was nothing more than forfeit
Begging for something far more
After all that has been conquered
One moment fearing the end
The next feeling secure again
This was not what was meant for her
She was perfectly built for torture
Yet she found a way out
A way to put away her self-doubt
That is a strength she did not see
One that fills her with glee
All it took was the focus changing to next step
And her bravery to finally take that leap
To believe she was worth all offered
And no there was nothing stopping her

False Perfection

Self worth tarnished by years of abuse
There was a point that she accepted being used
To be a tool in other's peace
Doing all they please
All claimed she was worth more
Yet giving her respect a gruesome chore
Slowly she sits back and can see clearly
That none were truly worthy
Giving away a part of her, she could never get back
Smiling through every attack
Swearing she could survive it all
Begging herself to never fall
Head high and heart open wide
Always be first to swallow her pride
Compromise a false picture of perfection
Knowing under the surface was pure rejection
For her soul was pure enough to run dry
And wonder she hid when it was time to cry
To give into the moment of bitterness
Falling hyper speed into black abyss
Then ducting herself off again
Reminding herself of the war to be won

134

Warrior Soul

Life never promised ease
It offers constant difficulty
One battle won
Yet a bigger comes along
And she hopes it will end
At some point she won't have to pretend
That her will won't be tested
For once she can't be bested
To see the storm coming
And truly feel nothing
That it wouldn't phase her
And she could feel secure
All while knowing the chance is low
And into the fire she must go
Wanting to continue the fight
And again make the balance right
Moving forward against the odds
Knowing rest is when all is lost
Too many depend on her warrior soul
To help obtain their own control

Against The Odds

The cruelties pile against her
The weight spreading like cancer
Her anxiety takes her through the tour of doom
Her inevitable failure automatically assumed
She gathers what strength she has left
And quickly retreats to her safety net
Allowing for a time to be defeated
Her will to fight depleted
Knowing sometimes rest is needed to carry on
And there is no hope the demons will ever be gone
They have made her into a home
One leaving them free to roam
And within her the war never ends
She just manages to constantly defend
Her soul tattered and scarred
Yet she still lives with her heart
The need to complete another day
Is the challenge always faced
She must over come it all
It would be a waste for her to fall
Regardless of the odds
Eventually she will conquer the choking fog

Drowning

The girl is beyond lost
She has no care of the cost
The payment made never too far
Every mistake leaving a unique scar
Piece by piece she is torn apart
Until all that's left is a hollow heart
Feeling no true peace in life
Even when she held the title of wife
No place felt as a true home to her
She held no one to their word
Allowing the pain to keep her down
And knowing her weight was in the crown
There were no lines she wouldn't cross
As long as it meant pretending there was no loss
She wandered into the abyss
Expecting to find her bliss
And down that dark and twisted path
She finally felt true wrath
The unfairness stacking higher and higher
As the doubts and lies stoked the fire
She freely fell into them as though in a trance
Watching the world pass by at a distance
Hoping with every moment to just be numb
But that relief just would not come

Awakening

Darling your spark has not withered
Though through your veins the poison slithered
The darkness quickly took hold
She never noticed the process too bold
The way fear slowly crept away
And the panic could no longer stay
Her bravado took hold in new form
And none could imagine the building storm
The way her heart started to race
A new spark, with a refreshing taste
The need to disappear fading quickly
As you are reminded of those moments briefly
The pain subsides in unique ways
And she realizes it was just a phase
There was no doom over head
Nothing left in life to truly dread
The poisoned tongues completely silent
And for once a reprieve from constant violence
The woman had seen this hell through
No one could ever claim the victory untrue
For the obstacles she surpassed mounted higher
And the clock always down to the wire
But still she stood among all the rubble
Still vowing to never truly crumble

My Darling

If you could just see my darling,
How can I help the pace I am falling
The way you wrap me in your arms at night
Safe and secure as you hold me tight
Not knowing exactly how I missed this so long
The man of my dreams right there all along.
The patience and kindness speaks right to my soul.
And by your side I lose all control.
You tell me in ways more powerful than word.
And I keep striving everyday to show you your worth
For daily I find a thousand and one,
Ways to fall more in love with you just for fun.

True Strength

The silence begged to play with her doubt
The depression finally over its drought
It came flooding in as it washed her away
Nothing in life held more gravity
She let it take hold, feeling helpless
While everyone screamed "Why did you do this?"
None took into account
The internal battle starting to mount
The way her mind pointed out every mistake
Leaving every victory feeling fake
Is she stupidly told all the good inside
The depression could twist it to something to hide
The torment never-ending within her mind
Forcing her to for once be kind
Kind to herself for how she has failed
And pride in the fact that she prevailed
As much as the inner voice tried to end her
Her soul was one not to be conquered
Though many would love to count her out
There is just too much she has learned about
The fact that her eyes clear every time
Shows the true strength in her mind

Taking Hers

Nothing in the past could have prepared for this
The escape needed for the internal bliss
The ease with which the change came
From blazing inferno, to comforting flame
At one point she found chaos amusing
Now seeking a life more soothing
To not be driven into pain
Allowing for once to protest its claim
They all swore it was all she could be
That it was just her take on normalcy
When they saw her head held high
They worked double to break her pride
Chanting she is worthless
Deserving of no kindness
So she did all she could
To prove she was just misunderstood
For once she stopped asking
And went straight to taking

Sweet Patience

If life were easy more would make it
And lonely would have a chance to be shaken
The path traveled would be more smooth
And no one would have to fight to prove
A soul that's tattered, a heart that's drained
Life never promised more than pain
Holding close the struggle you face
A problem not solved by sweet patience
A trial not passed through in silence
How the cycle repeated time after time
And all demanded that she be fine
That the stone façade never flatter
And her soul be broken, forever altered
Life never claimed it would be an easy ride
The only demand is that she survive
Make it through every twisted path
And be strong enough to withstand their wrath
No other option presents itself
Just find a way to withstand the hell

His Patience

His smile was patient, his tone was kind
The way he reacted blew her mind
He didn't see the tattered soul
The little pieces gone, leaving holes
He didn't take time to count the flaws
There was no need to tally her loss
For what he saw was pure and sweet
And no others could compete
He told her daily he saw her good
And for once she felt understood
No man ever took that much time to learn
Respect from them, for her never earned
So having him finally invest
Put her insecurity to the test
In a beautifully intoxicating way
She no longer feared if he could truly stay
Finding the diamond in the rough
He did so gracefully, when others claimed it too tough

Moment of Peace

He answered her tears with kindness
Dissolving in moments the madness
His love had the power to calm
Like the most soothing of balms
His patience had no limit
And he didn't demand her forfeit
When all in the world felt without hope
He pointed out the logical, less twisted road
Reminding her daily to continue the fight
Refusing to allow her to extinguish the light
Seeing a side of her no one else could
And pointing out daily she is at heart good
Her purity was one he had to preserve
And for once he gave all she deserves
Never once denying her heart its fill
And standing beside her strong and still
None had the ability to do with such ease
All the simplicity needed to give her relief

Put to Rest

Fight like hell until victory is obtained
Keep your composure, stay maintained
The battle has left too many scars
Ones that seem to reach within too far
All could point out how broken she was
And his cruelty still has no cause
It only took her defiance
To bring about his cruel violence
So she finally chose to stand tall
Hear his anger and refuse to fall
Do not allow him power again
It was time to keep it all in
It was time to finally take her power back
Protect herself from constant attack
His anger could no longer touch her
Not with how she rebuilt her armor
One simple task for years pushed to the side
Constantly forced to swallow her pride
Keeping her head hung down in shame
All because she stupidly learned his name
No love lost between the two
A battle now won, hopefully the war too

145

Hopeless Man

She wished the calm could spread
That somehow she could clear his head
The doom he feels smothering
The end of the world just hovering
About to all come crashing down
And he cannot attempt to hide the frown
All she wishes the bad could just stop
That she could find a way for his heart not to drop
If she could just loan out some hope
As he was at the end of his rope
Maybe he could start the climb
To get himself back to being alright
If he only knew the peace he offered
The way his presence always lifted her
His voice brought a smile long forgotten
His patience one she never was offered
To hear of his pain broke her soul
Especially when she just wanted him to feel whole

Behind Closed Doors

Love the breaking of a thousand lies
Understand seeing through the disguise
The fact he didn't belittle at first
That in the beginning her silence filled his thirst
No one could see the damage being done
How hell came to life in their home
The door would slam the world out
And suddenly her safety was something to doubt
Those hands meant to hold her sweetly
Were the ones pushing her to her knees
The ones supposed to hold her up
Were the ones teaching her to be tough
He did not tolerate her weakness
There was never a strong enough defense
No locked door that held him back
No true withstanding safety from his attack
At one point acting calm and peaceful
But at a moments notice his rage came back in full
To the world her smile was sweet, soul was pure
Behind that door she was worthless, beatings a cure
But she quickly hid with shame
Daring not to tarnish his name
For love she gave all she ever had
Yet at the end of the day she just couldn't accept dead

Brave Face

Do not ask about every flinch
Or why raised voices make her twitch
Do not dissect every reaction from her
For then the lines may blur
The ones between persona and reality
And real messes up her anxiety
She holds tightly to the strong will
The one that at times is the most bitter pill
Some days she wants nothing more than to crumble
To go back to speaking barely above a mumble
Go unnoticed peacefully through life
To go back to the obedient wife
Then locked back in her own hell
None would bother to question the silent shell
They would believe in her bitter nature
And the questions would never touch her
Yes she flinches at sudden motion
Scars from her pure devotion
Please do not raise the volume unneeded
You will never understand his hatred when heated
Allow her the temporary fake bravado
One day it will be permanent, and less hollow

The Kind Soul

If they only saw the fear she faced down
The sheer determination not to drown
As he smothered her in guilt and shame
Calling her everything but her name
They saw a brightness and bought the light
None daring to see his might
The way he bled her oh so silently
Leaving nothing more than a memory
A woman broken by this harsh world
There was never a true end to her hurt
The glances burned through her easily
Making it impossible to hold her sanity
Hiding the pain as though it didn't exist
Knowing to show it would be a forfeit
That defeat is one she cannot take
Just hold as tight as she can to the fake
If she let it slip, just once he wins
And the shame is one that never gives in
It will bury her whole and leave her behind
Only because she dared to always be kind

Loving Him

Loving him she lost herself
Giving until there was nothing left
At odds with the pain hidden inside
She chose the safe route and let him hide
Protecting his reputation with her own shame
She failed to live up to the gifted name
That was the illusion upheld
And kept busy she never would dwell
There was no need to question
He claimed the purest intentions
So that draining of the soul was labeled "growing"
And she went along unknowing
His hatred disguised as help
And the building of secrets she couldn't tell
A week at home for bruises to fade
She did her best to keep to the shade
Blend with the background for safety
As he constantly challenged her sanity
The cycle ran on forever
From the moment she vowed life together
He took that vow and turned it dark
Simply an excuse to break her heart
The last time she wiped away tears and blood
All while he claimed it was for her good
So when he finally walked out
She stopped drowning in self doubt
She took her freedom as a release
A way to finally live not begging on her knees

The Broken Man

He came to her as the world crumbled
He was one of a few who didn't mumble
Holding out a shred of hope
Right before she lost all control
With each moment she believed a little more
And he quickly became truly adored
His attention bringing her peace
His arms a beautiful release
An unexplainable rightness
Felt in every tender caress
The words he just couldn't say
Spoken through his actions everyday
She waited through hell and back
To find the man she always lacked
The one he didn't know he was
And suddenly her heart had a cause
Showing him the beauty he holds
And not hesitating to be bold
Hoping with each word that passes her lips
He will start to see the truth in this
He is a dream come to life
And it took her by surprise
Wishing to mend what others left broken
So that he can live free and open
A moan of his worth deserves that much
For being so purely genuine is rough
So she continues to pour love into him
And maybe he can love her on a whim

Warrior

Regardless of the pain she rises
Her integrity never compromises
They can claim pieces of her soul
But never take it as a whole
There is no capturing an eternal flame
There is no hope to tame
The spirit of a warrior within her
She will always rise, conquer
There is no other way
She must always be okay
To finally give in would be cruel
It would mean allowing herself to be a tool
The world does not hold that right
So though drained, she will fight
She will not be cast aside
She has allowed too much to slide
Now is her chance to turn the tables
Leave the world in shambles
There is no more need to be weak
Time to shed the persona of meek
She will move mountains with her will
And the truth shall spill
Too long she took the weight
Now she chooses to separate
The fact from fiction
And cause a little friction

False Hope

Each new face promised peace
A new exciting release
Though as this started to pass
Each found reasons it could not last
Slowly taking back all care once given
And her heart became hidden
Far out of reach from the false hope
For that would give them control
Too many times she has been misled
From false intentions, naively unread
They preyed on the way her soul held dreams
Playing it out and claiming it fit their needs
At some point she became a burden
Ending inevitably with her hurting
Wondering at what point she would learn
That love was a bridge best burned
To travel that path left too many scars
And she was left with scraps of her heart
Only the shredded love she ruined again and again
Each time the downfall came after letting them in
At some point it will repeat one last time
And there will be nothing to find
No more hope left to search for
No mission she will have energy to conquer
That moment inching closer
As she barely grasps closure
The world deciding to prove
A heart like hers had everything to lose

Destiny

If the truth was clear, she couldn't see
If intentions were spelled out, she couldn't read
The confusion a constant state
Turning inward to self-hate
Chastising for again misunderstanding
For foolishly, recklessly falling
The end always right over head
Each day filled with new dread
What was once a bud of hope
Now is hanging at the end of the rope
One final debate to be had
And once again she will be left empty and sad
Always the last one to know
Doing her best to peacefully let go
Her soul screaming to fight
To for once make it right
But no amount of resistance will matter
For he wants life without her
Her soul once again too much to take
And the fear unable to shake
She knew what the problem was
But endlessly hoped to call life's bluff
At some point she will learn the truth
As if the events weren't enough proof
The universe has already been that cold
To make it perfectly clear she is meant to be alone

Expected Progress

Free from his grasp she should flourish
There should be a level of being nourished
But all she does falls short
Left with nothing good to report
She has made peace with failure
The fact no one will remember her
It has enveloped her in a cloud
One in which she is never allowed
To just be herself for a moment
Not with having to fully commit
To the idea of total empty
But she does her best to avoid pity
There is no room for that now
For it would demand she bow
Though she is beaten she stands
Never giving into demands
The defeat she carries is heavy
And she can no longer ignore the mocking
Making a point to at least survive
For she was already on the ride
No brakes to slam, no direction to change
Just the dark, twisted path to deranged
Though she must follow the unlit way
It was pure strength making her stay

Giving In

She finally learned to stand her ground
Done with accepting waiting around
He thought her patience had no limit
And that her love, she would always give it
Though in her heart she wanted to
The truth was she had better things to do
Why wait on calls that never come
Why believe words over what has been done
He explained it away with such ease
Until finally he was no longer her peace
She wanted him to just give in
Know that he was already forgiven
She did not hold any ill will
She had just finally had her fill
His heart was spoken for
And it was too obvious to ignore
Though that woman broke him
He just couldn't let new love in
So when doubt finally took over
Without hesitation he went back to her
Suddenly the bond worth mending
And the new love felt her will bending
If only he could have just believed
Over time his doubts would be relieved
But his doubt led to a retreat
And the new love admitted defeat
Hoping the path he chose right
As she knew she had given up the fight

The Illusion

Did she tell you that she needed your love
Did she finally put you above
This time did she vow faithful
This time did she mention loyal
What promises could she have made
What promises kept were displayed
You claim to want to know the questions
You claim to stick to original intentions
I wonder if I misread the signs
I wonder if I finally lost my mind
For loving you felt beautifully safe
For loving you gave me all I could crave
So you pulling away was a total surprise
So you pulling the plug causing an uprise
Did you not see me start to glow
Did you not see the sparkle of hope
I barely got to show you the love I had
I barely got to start to erase the bad
Why was it so damn easy
Why was it impossible to love me
Were my flaws just too heavy
Were my flaws beyond scary
Just explain the process
Just explain away our mess
You pretended just long enough
You pretended to be mentally tough
How did she just come back in
How did she convince you to love again

The Process

In the midst of chaos she rose
Walking a twisted path she chose
All the times she gave herself up
Hoping to finally be enough
It was finally time to put that aside
And dig deep to her pride
Taking the courage to finally stand
Refusing to follow commands
If they were worthy time would tell
She was leaving their custom built hell
No longer focused on proving herself
Putting the expectations on the back shelf
It was a new stage in life
One riddled with frequent strife
The battles ahead daunting
The history that built her haunting
There was no sense denying she stumbled
But she walked on always humbled
Taking in the mistakes made as lessons
Never hiding from truthful confessions
To make progress she must allow change
A concept terrifying and out of range
Some days she gets lost in the course
Others she conquers, no remorse
There is no pause on the hurdles
In order to succeed, she must overcome obstacles
So head held high she faces each day
Knowing with strength all will be okay

158

Redefine

Falling victim no longer her path
Solid ground just within grasp
She must stand tall
She must not fall
Nothing in life meant to be easy
But gathering strength means victory
So though beaten, she will rise
There is no room for compromise
The soul must remain untouched
This healing process unrushed
If they saw the countless cracks
They would all be taken aback
None understood the pain she buries
Never showing the strength it takes to carry
She moves forward with no choice
Slowly finding her voice
The route to her truth twisted
But the cloud of doom lifted
In sudden light she is reminded
And faced with the beauty, blinded
There is purpose left for her
There are battles she can conquer
She does not have to remain beaten down
It is time to embrace the crown
Walk forward with pride
Away from the wreckage of a hellish ride
It is time they all finally see
As she embraces her inner queen

Fresh Start

Acting as a guide on their path
Finally a goal within grasp
Though she has failed many times
Still a true hero in their eyes
The love so pure between them all
A strong bond that will never fall
Waking each morning being needed
No longer allowing herself to be defeated
Their smiles bringing new hope to each day
Letting her know it will all be okay
Their innocence unable to hide
And she straps in for the ride
They depend on her to be strong
And she refuses to do them wrong
She will prove to them her love
Fix the broken, and rise above
One day they all will be able to look back
And take pride in getting on track
Together they will always manage
To walk away less damaged

Limbo

Pulling her back just as she walks
Her head just spins from the talks
Does he want to build their future
Could he truly love her
The doubts come running through her mind
One moment he is cold, the next kind
She balances in a sudden limbo
Knowing she should, but can't let go
He has proven just how little he cares
Just in his refusal to be there
He counts on her devotion to never waver
But ending it would do her a favor
Maybe if he finally just walked away
She would be able to see it more clearly
But each time she tries to make that call
He plays a card, makes her fall
And there she sits waiting again
Knowing she shouldn't, counting on him
She wishes for a moment to put it to rest
Why does his love feel like a test
And if she does fail, what will it mean
Will she finally be out of the in-between
The cycle won't end, he won't let it
And in the end she knows she'll regret this

Giving In Part 2

Caught in a war within herself
Knowing it will end in hell
Loving him already a battle
And she is left rattled
He argues that he never lied
Yet she is constantly left to cry
Never for sure what he means
To say he doesn't want her, while begging please
She attempts to walk away
And he asks her again to stay
This back and forth draining her soul
Wishing for once to turn cold
If only it was that easy
Just let go of him completely
Yet his smile draws her in
And his words, sweetly spoken
That is all it truly took
And she was caught back on his hook
The bond strong enough to fight for
But she knows he doesn't love her
He will never be able to commit
So she forces herself to forfeit
He can take his life back for good
She is done being just a mood
One he slips in and out of
As though she is unworthy of love

The Role

Innocently offering her all
Caught off guard as it dissolved
He made her believe for once
Now she feels more like a dunce
Once again making excuses for him
Hoping in the end she could win
When reality finally became clear
He was once again no where near
The unspoken promises broken
And she is left exposed and open
Just an example for the world
This is how to be beautifully hurt
Allow a man to twist and tangle
Let him leave you mangled
Do not ask him for true loyalty
Do not question dishonesty
Be prepared to play the fool
Follow his every rule
That is the only way to be
For otherwise he is unhappy
And the moment it happens he walks
No reasoning, no compromising talks
Just an empty space in her bed
And a million questions in her head
Ones that will never be answered
Not after this total disaster

Afflicted

Sleepless nights take over her life
As the pain twists like a knife
At one point he swore it could work
But she realizes those are only words
Never meant to hold true
And she must start anew
So one step at a time she leaves
No more time to grieve
The world will not end today
And she cannot retreat to the shade
It feels like safety but is a trap
It takes her potential and places a cap
The limitations start to flood in
And she has to fight through again
The other side so far away
But she must reach it you see
For mental torment never stops
And her heart almost pops
The cycle will continue endlessly
Never recovering from the empty
What would it possibly take
To make a happy ending real, not fake
What did she miss each time
What exactly was she crime
How does she start to fill the space
Needing answers, pleading her case
Love her or let her be
She cannot live in uncertainty

Sunrise

Birds chirping breaks the silence
And the day starts with new brilliance
A beautiful hope dares to bloom
That soon there will be an end to the doom
The shadows shrinking away
As the sun timidly takes its place
Slowly taking hold of more pride
Each graceful move shining more bright
The victory once again reached
Another night withstanding the siege
So hope blooms rapidly as darkness retreats
Nature calling out the transformation, so sweet
A splash of color spreads through the sky
An instant renewal, without much "try"
That vibrant beacon providing a rush
If appreciated it can provide grounding, being in touch
This fresh state a chance at change
Showing that anything is in range
The sweetness of dawn breaking
Should give courage to keep fighting
The privilege to once again awaken whole
And have the chance to regain control
If seen as an opportunity
The process is breathtaking
Just as the sun banishes the dark
Take that as a sign, you'll leave your mark

The Dreamer

The dreams that kept him up at night
Always feeling they were just out of sight
The risk of failure setting a limit
One between giving his all and complete forfeit
Holding the balance ever so delicately
Afraid of what may happen if he believed
The dream does not wither or waste away
It just stays there rooted, beckoning
Whispering to the soul within
To have a little hope and listen
The dreams won't fall silent, begging to be lived
All he needs to add is some hope and grit
Pushing through all the doubt inside
Deciding for once to believe in the light
There is no rule dictating dreams don't come true
And there is no crime in hoping they do
Following the path though easy, is boring
The soul needs the dream, for true exploring
Failure may come as a harsh reality
Then again so could success and self-actuality
Following the dream may lead to himself
If ever brave enough to not dwell
To escape the limits his mind built
And follow the dream without guilt
Some have found a way
It just takes silencing the inner dismay

Hidden Strength

Forcing doubt into the deep
Finding some strength she can keep
If only she moved slowly forward
Refusing to live as a coward
Life was far from gentle
Her soul completely dismantled
Though broken she stands
Finally done following demands
Taking power in survival
As she plots her revival
There is no knight rushing in
There is only her will to win
Relying only on her power
To make it through this dark hour
For in the big picture of life
That is how to label her strife
A moment that will pass soon
And once over give her soul more room
To grow further into the warrior
Giving a pause to all who questioned her
They may have knocked her down
But will beg mercy on the come around
Their doubt fire in her veins
She is reminded how to regain
Regain unwavering respect
Regain the strength to stand alone
Regain the ability to be her own "home"

Rise Up

You have no clue the unseen scars
None can see under the surface that far
She kept her guard up always
Knowing she couldn't allow it to fade
If any saw the damage done
It would seem as if he truly won
That was a price she refused to pay
She was unwilling to give him his way
As he spoke of her weakness with a smirk
She continued to brush off the dirt
What he claimed was far from true
And she did her best to continue to prove
That the strength was not drained
The soul was not fully stained
That her heart could be mended
If she only pretended
Just long enough to believe once again
To give hope another chance to come in
The scars are permanent, the trauma is not
A factor in life she almost forgot
Losing herself would have been easy
To just let it go completely
But her soul demanded a fight
To once and for all make it right
Find the courage to stand tall
But never forget this brutal fall

Run

The voice urges her to run
And she rushes to get it done
No longer willing to wait it out
Taking power from self doubt
The instinct says it is unsafe
And she refuses to stay in place
Taking the voice as a sign
There was nothing good to find
He claimed to be "acting" cold
But that lie was too bold
How could he claim it a defense
Treating her with no sense
Every order bluntly barked
Ignoring she was already scarred
He claimed ignorance of her past
As a means to justify his attack
She almost wanted to believe
To once again be deceived
But the voice refused silence
Mocking her with prior violence
So again she gathers her things
And takes escape as a blessing
Maybe a bit too cautious
But she will never take that risk
She will demand respect daily
And slowly regain her dignity

The Vow

Fear kept her silent for years
Pride kept her hiding the tears
Her vows kept her in place
And his hand kept bruises on her face
Their love beyond long gone
Reminded of all her wrongs
The self doubt ran too deep
And her sanity hard to keep
She slowly gave pieces away
The price to make him stay
Year by year she began to vanish
A sacrifice she barely managed
A duty she committed to fully
As he continued to increase his cruelty
The coldness spread within her soul
And she started to fight for control
Just one plea every so often
Doing her best to remain softly spoken
Still his anger was fueled
And she was left beaten and used
Knowing this went beyond her duty
That he didn't love her truly
Her fight became more forceful
Plotting an escape from his cruel
Just pushing enough to break free
Understanding for once the need
Life should not be lived hopeless
Realizing she deserved more than this

Self Reclaimed

The sparkle faint in her eyes
Dulled from all the believed lies
Yet not fully erased
Somehow her loving nature escaped
Moving forward with a few more dents
Cherishing that is the only expense
She has the chance to do more
Live life in constant adventure
See the mystery that once was
And finally find her true cause
The light within her unique
And she finds the will to speak
Finally over being silenced
Sick of reliving the violence
Thought he did all he could
He failed to end her good
The beauty within her will not leave
Although he filled her with nothing but grief
She made a point to barely survive
Until the time came to take back her life
The sparkle shone brighter than ever before
As the anger began to ignite within her
Now that it started there will be no pause
And one day he will realize his loss
By then the regret will be too deep
For his pride to admit his defeat
He played the game and lost the prize
And she started regaining herself in strides

The Dance

If you look too long she may break
Afraid you see every slight mistake
The way she hiccups over a simple hello
And she constantly offers to go
Believing that her presence was a burden
Giving in to the need to stay hidden
The inner compass begging her to run
Never take the risk of coming undone
Criticizing herself for every move
Always feeling the need to prove
Some how over and over falling short
Just staying unclear the impact of her effort
Anyone who spoke of her only presented flaws
And those wounds have yet to scar
Being ripped back open with each remark
Already putting doubt in her heart
Could she really rise above this
Was her character even worth it
The questions always background noise
And she slowly loses more and more choice
Do as they demand her to
Be the doll always ready to start anew
Quickly being stripped to nothing
The cycle always repeating
The fear of rejection keeping her
A willing volunteer to the torture
Self-doubt chanting endlessly
And still she spins, dizzily

The Cure

If falling had a cure there would be hope
A possible way to end suffering and cope
The path would suddenly clear
And she could finally start to steer
The life she craved, beyond herself
A long gone dream high on the shelf
If she had just focused on that
She could have completed her task
To be the woman they finally valued
If such a concept could be true
That being decreased with every blow
And the shame would free flow
She bowed to society's narrow demands
Blindly following constant commands
Be a lady, sit correct, be seen not heard
Bombarded by every cutting word
Her worth built by a twisted society
Never wanting to view her clearly
She dutifully followed the ideal
Into a nightmare turned real
She thinks once again on the path taken
And the precious dreams forsaken
All she hoped for was an end
To his unrelenting anger, before she had to bend
A way to erase the cruel mark
Of a love abandoned in the dark
If she could just find the cure, and heal
She may dare once again to feel

Remember

She remembered her strength over the years
All of the overcome tears
She reminded herself she was better than this
That she could find true bliss
She thought of everything she got through
And decided she could get through this too
She picked herself up
And remembered she could be tough
There is a fire within her
And no one could stop her growing power
Shortly after the greatest fall
She finally realized she wasn't broken after all

Reformify

The escape was planned she claims
And yet she fails to forget the names
The ones who crossed the line
Without regret in all their lies
They saw no wrong in the deceit
As they plotted her defeat
But have the nerve to question
How dare she even mention
The level of punishment withstood
Slowly erasing the amount of good
If they ignore the pain inflicted
The shame won't fully sink in
Yet the thought still lingers
What if they never broke what was hers
If the damage was never done
What would she have become
The truth is they built her stronger
From weak to pure survivor
They aimed at her soul unrelenting
And in the end she stopped accepting
Never again will the soul be under fire
The weight no longer a desire
She moves past all the dark
And quickly encases her heart
Protecting against the mere chance
To once again be victim to circumstance
She will never be that fool
Its no longer worthwhile to be a tool

Keep Up Appearances

Try not to see the broken pieces
Try not to see all that she needs
The damage done will not erase
And that smile held tightly in place
The strength cannot begin to falter
Her course will not be altered
Do not attempt to save her now
Just know your place and dutifully bow
She is a queen before you standing tall
All the while being commanded to fall
Show some weakness, hell just cry
And once again they rush in with their pride
Fools boasting about the wisdom earned
As though she was of any true concern
They demanded she take it all in
Follow their guide out of her sin
None gave her the time to explore
Her sense of adventure, a thing to ignore
Keep it tucked down deep
It is a shameful secret to keep
Do not talk of wandering off
To those without imagination, it sounds like lost
Speak of a plan that fits their wishes
Keep obedience from being his Misses
Questions cause problems don't you know
So ask nothing, just let it go
Play the part they all want to see
And when no one is looking dare to be free

Gained Wisdom

Do not give into despair my dear
Do not live paralyzed by fear
Things are never as bleak as believed
Do not allow yourself to be deceived
If fighting is in your nature
That is the instinct to nurture
Now is the time to build defenses
And test daily your reflexes
For the war to come is brutal
And kindness at this point futile
I should know, I'm still healing
My war almost left me unfeeling
Each battle fought taking more
In the end I was stripped to my core
Each belief I held shattered
All my merit never mattered
Only my will to survive held value
This isn't to scare, but prepare you
For once the rebellion is detected
You will surely be labeled defective
Shortly after the criticism will rain
Know fighting it will not be in vain
I have waded deeper into the dark
Willing the fates to tear me apart
Yet I still move forward
No longer needing to cower
That is the prize to this ordeal
The beautiful freedom to finally heal

Awakening

This smile won't fade
He brought out the happy place
He made her feel worthy
Never rushed or in a hurry
They could sit in silence peacefully
Who knew she could be this happy?
His arms felt like security
He quickly made quiet all her worries
He pushed her limits with tenderness
To the point she craved his caress
For too long she felt like slipping away
Now she just hopes she can stay
A sweet and fresh beginning
Another chance at a happy ending

His Smile

Slowly he gives her more
And she can peek through the door
She got a glimpse of his pride
A genuine smile he couldn't hide
And in that moment she fell
Her heart wanted to hear everything he could tell
The silly stories that made him cringe
The tragic ones that made his heart twitch
She wanted to know this man like no other
She just hoped he could want her
In his eyes she saw the need
But his warning she attempted to heed
But his smile pulled her in
And her heart and mind were racing
He had no clue the parts he had awakened
Or how her world was taken
One day he may get to see
How he rescued the pixie

179

Calming Demons

He made sleep safe
And her heart quake
The night terrors vanished with ease
And it was relieving to be so pleased
She heard her giggle again
And she couldn't hold it in
He touched a part of her left dormant
And now the hope runs rampant
She reminds herself to slow down
But her heart beats so loud
Her smile seems brighter and more real
He gave her something she could feel
The doubt is still there
But with each passing day it becomes less of a scare

The Escape

Underestimated at first sight
They all assumed her nature
Believing she would run, not fight
All counting down the days to her departure
A beast within not many saw
Awoken by the sudden need to defend
They all highlighted every flaw
And yet to her face all pretend
The love given just a running tab
A condition she was obligated to meet
Presented as if on a slab
Just another tasty piece of meat
Her soul matters very little in their eyes
And her protests soon fell silent
It was her duty to compromise
Or else they would become violent
Life was not as once pictured to be
There was no hope left to hold
The hope to, just once, be free
Was just far too bold
So she kept silent about her dreams
Never hinting at the beauty
A sudden escape from extreme
The never-ending, blood-thirsty cruelty
Her mind had a space made of plans
Little scenarios she compiled through the years
This space addressed all of her demands
This space was safe, when she was overcome with fear

Hollow

The pain stands deadly still
Easing closer to finish the kill
Sinking deeper into the shadows
As the feeling spreads, hollow
To rebuild takes strength yet gained
And so the choice is what method to numb the pain
Which vice will carry the weight of the night
Which will erase the memory of each fight
Blow by blow the past replays
As if approved by the fates
The lesson never learned
Leaving the soul open for more hurt
Tell the tale of bravery in silence
Just leave out the brutal violence
Do not speak of the days of misery
How accepting defeat felt easy
Just lay down and let go
None of it must ever show
There was no fix to the hell lived
And no demand for her to forgive
Just move forward a bit tougher
Be grateful that life was rough on her
Thank the fates for the pain
Appreciate the strength gained
That is the demand that always follows
Refusing to let her give into the hollow

Be Kind

You built her up to do anything
Then crushed her slowly into nothing
You told her to be smart, be bold
But apparently that grew tiresome and old
For now you beg her to hush her mind
That no matter what she must always be kind
Even when others act so cruel
Do her best to stay level
Yet as she repeats the lessons taught
She feels as though there were some forgot
Where is the one about stand her ground
What about the idea to not back down
Wasn't there one about owning respect
How anything less was an instant reject
She grasps at traces of the braveness in her
As the black and white of it all starts to blur
See you use kindness to mean accepting
Her behavior measured by how much she is letting
Letting you use her, and break her at times too
If she does as you please what needs improved
But her mind still wanders to that far off place
Just as the smile flees her face
Remember girl there was once a time
Where it was okay to fight back
And not be "kind"

Walk On

Oh how things have changed
As she was at the edge of deranged
No one saw her surviving this
It was just too much to accomplish
Daily she read doubt in their eyes
She could see through the empty lies
What was left unsaid spoke volumes
And quickly diminished her inner value
Until she chose to finally stand up
And take that final step to being tough
To decide she had to be capable
To make her life truly full
So she went from timid and weak
To refusing not to speak
Telling all the horror she survived
And holding her head high
She waded through the storm to the other side
Cringing at memories of the gruesome ride
Promising herself to never again
Allow anyone to destroy her from within
Suddenly she finds a life she can boast about
One that won't flood her with self-doubt

Changed Behavior

He used to count the tears
And shelter from the fears
He used to pay attention
His love never to question
She knew he would always be there
Even when she was uncontrollably scared
That's the role he always played
Until the new him came to stay
The one who ignored the hurt
And drug her morals through the dirt
She couldn't get a passing glance
He held a guarded stance
She pleaded and begged
For him not to forget
But just like that his love was gone
And in its place a heart of stone
No matter how hard she tried, she couldn't reach him
And she knew it was time to finally give in

Healing

If you find her approach gently
Do not rush so boldly
The world has always come to quickly for her
And she still cannot begin to count the scars
Far too many have gone deeper than the surface
And she wonders silently how to end this
For years she hid within herself
Trying like hell to put terror high on a shelf
But it always found a way to the front lines
And she cringes knowing there is no rewind
Try as she might she can only move forward
Living with the damage left by a coward
Still being praised by so many
And she knows none of them can truly see
Why not to rush her into forced trust
That is such a cruel thrust
To be that openly vulnerable
Is something she is just incapable
Of achieving or even trying to assume
She is still recovering from his abuse
Her body is healed but her mind is broken
It will still be years for her learn to be open

Refuse to Fall

No one ever warned her it would be like this
That she could lose it all in one little slip
She always thought the process took much longer
And that by default she was much stronger
When it finally took hold she was blindsided
And by her own hand too weak to fight it
So the wave crashed over her unrelenting
The world moved on almost forgetting
The woman she once was long before
She gave up on her beautiful mind and endless power
She used to have so much fight within
But life lost all the hope her heart was given
Easily she saw only the scars and the pain
It was too much to see yet any wisdom gained
So defeated by life she refused to fight back
Letting all that she loved sli through the cracks
Once it was gone regret filled her soul
And she learned to never feel whole
Thinking it best to allow life to win she cowered
Until she was forced to once again remember her power
To stand and take the weight of it all
And once again refuse to back down or fall

Manipulator

He swore he would always love her
Then acted as though she could be conquered
Day by day attempting ownership
As is she came with a purchase slip
If she fought any of his rules
The manchild would be beyond cruel
She became worthless, a burden
Regardless of his mean, she was the one "hurting him"
So she fell as she could in line
And bit her tongue so she never "whined"
He twisted every action to suit his need
No measure too far to feed his greed
Always swearing his love was true
And she followed blindly with no clue
All his promises were empty
And his hold on her would destroy her completely
He crafted such a perfect storm
From which her destruction was born

Tug of War

She did her best to stay callous
To protect from further malice
The problem was his love was pure
And the lines started to blur
Between loving him an holding back
Always prepared for an attack
But he never even raised his voice
And the gentleness left her no choice
One day she swore never again
Next she knew she was fully in love with him
The way he looked at her with such care
Like he didn't see the unmistakable dare
"Love me and I will break you"
That was all she knew
Until he came into her life
And quickly erased all her strife
He showed her love she never knew
And proved that to her he could be true
She went from refusing love
To knowing he was the one she dreamed of
A real man was finally by her side
For him she would always be down to ride
He gave her a gift that was priceless
And he rescued her from her own mess
Her only hope was to be good enough
After he beautifully called her bluff

Rot

The battles she fought unseen
The scars still clear and mean
He swore a love he did not possess
And left her more than a mess
She went from capable to scared
And he would strip her so much more than bare
He filled her head with lies
And quickly drowned all of her cries
He swore she always provoked him
And this was a war she could not win
She cowered under his glance
Learning quickly a guarded stance
Each strike dealt earned
And for simple freedom, she yearned
None imagined the abuse he gave out
Until it was too late, and there was no more doubt
In that hospital bed she lay broken
And not a single accusation needed spoken
He had done this to her
Finally they saw her life of torture
So when she begged for an escape
All signed on with a part to play
When all was finally said and done
She no longer had to look back, for the war she had finally won
His hold on her broken but her spirit was not
And she moved on to a place where his cruelty
would no longer cause her soul to rot

Hollow

She has lived through things no one should
Merely because his ego said he could
Could demean her and cut her down
Could meet her every effort with a scowl or frown
He believed he had a right to strike her
For her the truth began to blur
So deep inside herself and home she would hide
Until the bruises would fade and subside
Hiding his inner monster her duty
One she performed diligently
To allow the facade to fall
Would be seen as a failure by all
So she clung to the hope no one knew
And each day his cruelty grew
At first it was merely harsh slaps
Then quickly it became vicious attacks
As the years passed she learned new tricks
Ways to keep allowing him to get away with it
Bruises on her neck from his fingers, covered by a shawl
But how exactly do you hide a broken jaw?
Months hidden inside of course, that was how
And over the years she learned always cower, always bow
He would smirk when she praised him for others
And if her voice trembled while saying it none seemed bothered
They accepted her lies so easily fed
As he quietly pushed her closer to the edge
Until finally they realized she was but a shadow
Of the woman she was, thanks to him....she was hollow

Beautiful Warrior

Don't you know not to believe his lies
The ones spread for my demise
The ones that said I was not enough
When all could see I called his bluff
The way he held me was not a gift
And all his sweetness would quickly shift
When I finally ran I had no brakes
For I had endured all I could take
I took the beatings, I took the pain
Until freedom was all I hoped to gain
Just the chance to stand tall
And for once not be forced to fall
To move on and find a man gentle and kind
For in life you cannot rewind
The hurt I lived would not erase
The best I could do is take the wisdom gained
Knowing deep down never again
Would I live a life where monsters win
He may have kept me once upon a time
And in that moment I walked the jagged line
But once those ties were broke
My voice grew stronger with each time I spoke
Spoke of his malice and his deceit
Until I realized the monster was truly beat
None could stop me from being bold
And my beautiful story wasn't over, and could still be told
The beginning tragic as none could deny
But the beautiful warrior I became none could defy

Echoes

They tell her time heals all wounds
That her suffering will end soon
Still she demands to know exactly when
Will the eternal torment finally end
When will the nightmares stop replaying
All the hateful things he loved saying
When will the echoes of doors slamming
Not remind her of the time of her reckoning
When will she be okay with the word baby
And not have it bring back the whole calamity
When will sleep come easily
Not be something hardest to reach
When will peace be a given
Not a mystical ride no longer ridden
When will safety be her for the taking
Not be distraught or always shaking
She wonders all these things and much more
As they swear there is nothing left to conquer
They claim all her battles have been fought
And the pain she lived can be forgot
But the echoes still sound within her soul
Where she is left less than whole
So she again begs to know when
Can she finally say she actually is free of him
They tell her now and forever
That's when she realizes the echoes may be too much to conquer

His Love

His eyes a crystal clear blue
Stare at her with a love so true
He holds her in a warm embrace
And gives her his everything with grace
He knows her heart needs healing
To be taught how to be truly feeling
So with the patience of a saint he guides her
And time asses in a beautiful blur
Each kiss holds an unspoken promise
As he only gives the most gentle caress
She starts to forget the horrible past
Finally accepting this love will last
He never raises his voice or his hand
His love does not come with any command
Finally in life she feels safe
As he quickly found a way to erase
All of her doubts and all of her fears
Finally she is able to let him come near
In his arms she found a safe haven
The one thing in life she was constantly craving
He knew exactly how to properly treat her
And with him the world was theirs to conquer
He kept a beautiful smile on her face
And filled her heart with a love no one could replace
The miracle of his love was daunting at times
But she knew in her heart he would never cross the line
He was her saving grace so beautifully given
And with him she was finally safe enough to be truly living

Aftermath

Do you see the scars he left
Or the pain deep in her chest
The way she would hang her head in shame
Even years later, at the mention of his name
She pretended to be tougher than this
But her escape an unattainable bliss
He held her hostage in her mind
As she does her best to remain kind
Do not allow his cruelty to win
Do not give up and forfeit to him
She knew better that to quickly bow
That was a sin she mustn't allow
His hatred seeps deeply under the surface
And she knows she must escape this
She must prove stronger than his hate
To finally rejoice in no longer being his mate
He moved on once she was deemed broken
He left her lying there pitifully choking
She thought for sure she would never survive
She wouldn't even dare to hope she could thrive
She was trained to believe she was a mere nothing
Just a pathetic attempt, a meaningless fling
So when she rebuilt she was more than just shocked
And she vowed one day his world she would rock
She waited patiently, silently plotting
Knowing once the time came she would not be forgotten

Monsters

They told her monsters weren't real
But the damage they did, she could definitely feel
She whispers they can be if you look
And not simple the ones hidden within a book
The monsters she knew were men all around
The ones claiming she was perfectly safe and sound
The same men vowing to protect her
Would make her life a hellish blur
Worse still was the constant doubt
Every time she dared to speak out
The way they would dismiss each claim
How dare she defile his name
So she learned quickly to keep silent
To do everything in her power to hide the violent
To take all the pain and hide it within
Just do as he demanded and never question
She learned early on no one would believe
And that speaking up would get no relief
So she hid deep within herself
And put all feelings high on a shelf
Hidden away where no one could dare touch
And she kept pretending it was never too much
She swallowed self-hatred like a daily vitamin
Never seeing that truly it was her poison
Until one day she broke free from it all
And all at once their disguises crumbled, as
she stood victorious and proudly tall

Broken Words and Empty Thoughts

He said I love you
She thought he meant it
He said he would always be true
She thought she was selfish
He said she was his favorite pet
She thought it would last forever
He said she just had to forfeit
She thought it was safe, he would never
He said she was to blame
She thought she could change him
He said each step was to tame
She thought their future was more then a whim
He said he owned her
She thought that was a prize
He said the fight was a blur
She thought about how to conceal black eyes
He said he would stop the violence
She thought he was someone she could trust
He said her flaws made her deserve it
She thought her obedience was a must
He said she was unworthy, weak
She thought about all that she gave
He said he knew she would turn the other cheek
She thought of no longer being his slave
He said he would destroy her if she tried to leave
She thought for just a moment and then finally she fought

False Bravado

Tell me again how I won't survive
Announce to world I am too weak to thrive
Tell them all how I am nothing
Just pathetic puppet on your strings
Claim to control me every action
That I exist merely for your satisfaction
Take pride in your never ending cruelty
To serve you, my only duty
Celebrate your full control
Laugh at knowing I will never again be whole
Strip me of all humanity
Boast on owning me fully
Convince yourself you have truly succeeded
That all your threats have been needed
Give yourself that false bravado
So it will shock you when I finally go
When I finally take that glorious stand
When I no longer cower at your commands
When I rebel against all you have taught
When I decide the battle is worth being fought
I want to leave you like you made me
All alone, pathetic, broken and weak
So go right ahead and puff out your chest
For in the end we will see who does it best

Consumed

She feels the walls closing in
How long must she ay for one sin?
Being cut from all she loves and adores
The pain far too much to ignore
Her heart and soul breaking
Her will to carry on shaken
She feels like she went to war and lost
Like she has been left behind and forgot
Dying inside a little more each day
Wondering if she will ever be okay
Life feels like an empty pit
As they all treat her like shit
They tell her she deserves this
And it's becoming hard not to crave that old numbness
Giving up a beautiful temptation
How exactly is she supposed to win?
All she wants is to be surrounded by her littles
Just a chance to meet in the middle
Needing to see their sweet faces
Knowing nothing can replace this
To fill that empty pit
And remind her not to forfeit
For now she just holds tight to the thread
Ans tries to avoid being consumed by the dread

What Love Costs

Your love cost me my friends
No let's start at the top
Your love cost me my heart
I gave it freely
Your love cost my trust
I willingly gave my all
Your love cost me my car
Ii know petty....but still
Your love cost my freedom
I stood behind it
Your love cost missing my grandpa passing
I missed being there for my dad like I strive for
Your love cost my loved ones to grieve my absence
They never deserved that
Your love cost missing my mother in laws passing
I wasn't there to hold my children through that
Your love cost 9 months of isolation
I had repeated mental breakdowns
Your love cost me to question everything
But I did it all for pure love
My love cost you to be honest
Insufficient funds
My love cost you to be my peace
"I forgot my wallet"
My love cost you commitment
"I get paid next week"
My love cost you to respect me
"Do you accept change?"
What I require is bare minimum given what Ii have paid
The issue is....you've always been bad at sticking to your budget

Letter of Resignation

And one day she just stopped
She stopped doing
Stopped caring
Stopped being
Stopped pretending
Stopped pleasing.....
She took a step back
And saw what she had become
Slowly she started to tear away
All the pieces she attached for aesthetic
She saw that she didn't need the disguise
And finally recognized her true beauty
She was done playing the jester
Felt the pressure lifting
Found peace by stepping away from the chaos
She took comfort in her strength
Once she stopped kneeling for others
Each day gaining momentum
Though the journey was grueling
She gave herself permission to survive
The lonelier it got, the more she invested into herself
Taking back the right to live, not just exist
She found a way to banish the need to be everyone's everything
Her circle became smaller as those against her faded away
And she finally felt free
In time she rebuilt the amazing woman she always was
And put action to the words
Darling, do not dim your light for other people's sensitive eyes.
And finally with her rediscovery
She glowed

When I Grow Up

The age old question
What do you want to be when you grow up?
Well, when I grow up, I want to be peace
For any struggling through the mess of life
When I grow up, I want to be comfort
For any why feel misplaced
When I grow up, I want to be patience
For all striving to make progress
When I grow up, I want to be compassion
For those who have ever lost their way
When I grow up, I want to be acceptance
For any who ever felt rejected
When I grow up, I want to be kindness
For those that just need one moment to change their day
When I grow up, I want to be safety
For those forced to weather the storms
When I grow up, I want to be gentle
For any this world has left broken
When I grow up, I want to be unconditional love
For all that have felt cruelty's kiss
When I grow up, I want to be a safe haven
For all the lost souls needing a soft landing
When I grow up, I want to be understanding
For those who are victim to life's twists
When I grow up, I want to be human
And always remind myself that others are as well
Now that I am grown
I understand all that I should strive for
The beauty is, life is constantly "growing up

Printed in the United States
by Baker & Taylor Publisher Services